# MAKING POOR MAN'S
# GUITARS

This book is dedicated to Roy H. Williams, who gave me Don Quixote's lance; Glenn Kaiser, who brought me to Blind Willie Johnson; and Ben Baker, who made sure we got a 12 pack of Budweiser before going to the greenhouse.

For Melissa, who is my everything.

Special thanks to David Sutton, Randy Flaum, William Jehle, RJ Gibson and the New Orleans Jazz Museum for their photo contributions.

All photographs are by the author unless otherwise noted.

---

© 2018 by Shane Speal and Fox Chapel Publishing Company, Inc., 903 Square Street, Mount Joy, PA 17552.

*Making Poor Man's Guitars* is an original work, first published in 2018 by Fox Chapel Publishing Company, Inc. No part of this publication may be reproduced, stored in a retrieval system, or transmitted, in any form or by any means, electronic, mechanical, photocopying, recording, or otherwise, without the prior written permission of the publisher and copyright holders.

ISBN 978-1-56523-946-3

Library of Congress Cataloging-in-Publication Data

Names: Speal, Shane, author.
Title: Making poor man's guitars / Shane Speal.
Description: Joy, PA : Fox Chapel Publishing Company, Inc., [2018] | Includes
   index.
Identifiers: LCCN 2018023294 (print) | LCCN 2018025101 (ebook) | ISBN
   9781607655473 (ebook) | ISBN 9781565239463 (softcover)
Subjects: LCSH: Cigar box guitar--Construction. | Musical
   instruments--Construction.
Classification: LCC ML1015.G9 (ebook) | LCC ML1015.G9 S658 2018 (print) | DDC
   784.192/3--dc23
LC record available at https://lccn.loc.gov/2018023294

To learn more about the other great books from Fox Chapel Publishing, or to find a retailer near you, call toll-free
1-800-457-9112 or visit us at *www.FoxChapelPublishing.com*.

We are always looking for talented authors. To submit an idea, please send a brief inquiry to
acquisitions@foxchapelpublishing.com.

Printed in Singapore
First printing

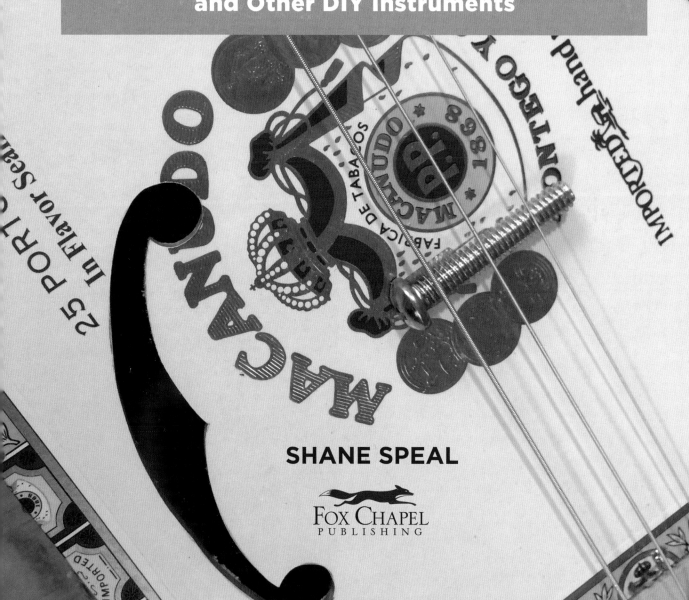

# MAKING POOR MAN'S
# GUITARS

## Cigar Box Guitars, the Frying Pan Banjo, and Other DIY Instruments

**SHANE SPEAL**

**FOX CHAPEL**
PUBLISHING

# CONTENTS

PHOTO: RANDY FLAUM

PHOTO: DAVID SUTTON

# Introduction

If I were to write just a book on building guitars, it would merely be an instruction in carpentry. If I were to add the rich history behind the instruments, the book would certainly have a bit more depth. However, I am neither a carpenter nor a professional historian; I am a musician who, to paraphrase the composer Harry Partch, was *seduced into carpentry and history* from searching for the sounds in my mind.

If I don't talk about the music, then it is all a worthless quest.

It's always about the music—a deeper music.

As I write this, my ears are still ringing and my voice is hoarse from attempting an old Cab Calloway song during band practice tonight. (Or was it the AC/DC cover?)

My band was at my place, running through a few song ideas. The mutant group, Shane Speal & the Snakes is built around cigar box guitars, washtub basses, homemade percussions, and a harmonica. All plugged into Spinal Tap amps and playing at breakneck speeds. In tonight's practice, we experimented with a new sound by feeding the harmonica through a beer can microphone into a 1970s rotating Leslie organ speaker. It was fantastic!

When fans ask us about our genre, we usually just stand there and give them blank stares, because we have no clue. We're a jug band that plays hard blues. Or blues-meets-Motorhead on homemade instruments along with a toilet paper gun and confetti cannons.

Maybe the genre is "jug fusion" or "trash rock." Regardless of a tidy name, we're dangerous.

I believe music should be dangerous, on-the-edge, a little sloppy, and most of all, *human*. I attribute this philosophy to what I heard on a live, bootleg Sex Pistols cassette in 1982. I was twelve and just beginning to grow my mullet, cranking music on my stereo. To me, the Sex Pistols were the epitome of rock and roll with a jug band attitude. Sid couldn't play bass, but he still did. Rotten couldn't sing, but there he was, center stage, screaming with a beady-eyed glare. Jones and Cook were a freight train together. It shouldn't have worked, but it did.

Cigar box guitars really shouldn't work, but they do—magnificently. They're the only instrument I use in my band.

Shane Speal & the Snakes plays mostly dive bars in rural Pennsylvania. Our fans follow us in hardcore devotion from show to show, because they never know what's gonna happen at the next gig. When you play 100% homemade instruments, something is bound to get destroyed at any moment. There are always two rolls of duct tape on stage just in case a repair is needed.

Add the fact that we never use a set list. The entire three-hour concert is spent wrestling uncompromising instruments and feeding off the audience's energy. Our shows sometimes contain reworked songs as diverse as Blind Willie Johnson, Jimi Hendrix, Muddy Waters, Depeche Mode, and Led Zeppelin. Some nights our songs are developed on the spot.

And there's always danger ahead. The gig is either a masterpiece or it's a train wreck. One night, a bar had a blackboard in the bathroom where somebody scrawled: "This band is HORRIBLE!" Another person scratched out "HORRIBLE" and wrote "AWESOME." And THAT completely sums up my music.

So what is this all about? Why cigar box guitars with their out-of-tune janglings? Why gutbucket basses and their warbling thuds?

As you dig into this book, you'll realize it's not a gimmick for me.

It's my life.

There are two types of projects in this book. The first lists all the parts, tools, and instructions, along with photos. The second is Builders' Diaries, which chronicle unique instruments that were created in the past, usually on a whim, and were designed without any structured plan. I include them here to inspire you to try your own inventions.

# Foreword

PHOTO: GREG LAMBOUSY, THE NEW ORLEANS JAZZ MUSEUM

**Little Freddie King's Cigar Box Guitar: A Bluesman's Firsthand Account**

On January 17, 2017, I had the opportunity to interview 77-year-old blues legend Little Freddie King on stage at the New Orleans Jazz Museum and learn about the cigar box guitar he built when he was only six years old. King's face lit up when we talked and every detail was as vivid in his memory as if it just happened earlier that day.

*Me: I hear that when you were a little kid, you started out making your own instruments.*

**Little Freddie King:** For sure, because I was so poor, I couldn't afford to buy my own guitar.

*Me: Where were you living and how old were you at the time?*

**L.F.K.:** Macomb Mississippi. I was six years old.

Now, my dad, he used to play all the time. He'd get off from work and come straight home and run up on the porch and go in the living room to the far corner and pick his guitar up and run back on the porch. He'd sit in his special rocking chair and would start a-rockin', playing guitar. I said, "Daddy, why don't you learn me how to play?"

He said, "Boy, I can't learn you how to play, but I can show you three chords and you have to learn yourself how to play."

My dad used to work up in the Mississippi Delta, he'd go up there and pick cotton. While he was goin' up there, I was getting real busy taking his guitar from the corner and banging on it, trying to learn how to play. I kept bangin' on his guitar, and I broke a string on it. I said, "Uh oh, I know I got it coming now!"

So here he come that evening, wide open and running there, grab the guitar and back to the front porch and jumped in his rocking chair. He banged down on it . . . and there was no string at the bottom—not as many notes, you know? He said, "Boy, get here!"

I said, "Uh oh." [Laughs] I said, "What's the matter, Daddy?"

He said, "You know what's the matter! You done broke my damn guitar!"

I said, "What? I didn't do that, Daddy!"

He said, "Boy, don't you lie to me. Come here." He went and got a rattan vine. Man, I tell you the truth, when he finished me with that rattan vine, that learnt me not to fool with his guitar anymore!

So I said, "I'm gonna have to do something to get me a guitar. I ain't gonna fool with his guitar anymore because he'd likely kill me."

In the next couple days, my mama said to me, "Sonny, you wanna go to the store for Mama?"

I said, "Yeah, Mama."

So she sent me to the store . . . Where I'm from, they only had gravel roads . . . So here comes two big shots in an Eldorado Fleetwood Cadillac . . . dust was flyin' . . . When the dust settled, I saw they tossed something out the window. I looked down in a ditch and it was a cigar box.

I said, "Wow, that's just what I need to make my own guitar so I won't have to get no whoopin' no more!" So I get down in the ditch and get that old cigar box out of there and go on home.

I said, "Now I got to make my own guitar."

I got to thinkin' that I didn't have no saw or mechanical tools or carpentry tools to build with. So I crushed an old Coca Cola bottle [to make a homemade knife] and whittled me a round hole in the center of it.

Then I said, "I got to paint it and glue it together," but I didn't have none of that nor money to do it, so I went to this pine tree that's got that rosin coming out of it. So I got some rosin and put it in a cup, put it on the stove, and melted it. Then I went to the chimney . . . that had soot that was black, and I took that and melted with the rosin. And it made it black. [Using the cooked rosin concoction], I glued it together and painted it black.

I said, "What am I going to do for the neck and the frets?"

So around the house, we had a picket fence. So I ran out there and grabbed a picket and snatched it off the fence and took the same piece of glass and whittled it down. Then I put it on the cigar box. So then I said, "I got to make the frets." I thought about the hay wire outside. So I went out and got some hay wire, the smallest hay wire I could find. I took it, cut it, and glued it down on the "keyboard." I then took another piece of wire to the stove and got it red hot and then marked the holes at the end of [the headstock] to make my tuners.

I said, "Now I got my cigar box guitar, but I don't have no strings!" So my daddy came for lunch and he used to make this homemade corn liquor called "buck." You drink a pint of that and you'll be drunk for seven days! And so he'd go back there and get charged up on that buck and he tied the horse to the pole. And the horse started stomping and kickin' his tail as he was swatting horse flies. And I heard the sound of his tail moving in the air. "Woosh! Woosh! Woosh!"

I said to myself. "He made that tail sound through the air, so I wonder what it would sound like on my guitar."

I went out to the horse and he looked at me. I said "I ain't gonna bother you. I just want to take a hair and see what it will do on my guitar." So I pull

Born Fread Eugene Martin in 1940, Little Freddie King has been a pillar of the New Orleans music community since moving there in 1954. A cousin of Lightnin' Hopkins, King's style mixes country blues with the fierce electric blues of his namesake, Freddie King.

one strand out. I put that on [the guitar] and it made a sound. So I went back to the horse and he looked at me again. I said, "I'm back again and I want five more strings from you, horse." So I kept pullin', pullin', pullin' till he had a great big bald spot in his tail! [Laughs!]

I just wished I would have been able to hold onto that guitar until today.

*Special thanks to Collins Kirby of the New Orleans Cigar Box Guitar Festival and Greg Lambousy and the staff of the New Orleans Jazz Museum for making this interview possible.*

# CHAPTER 1: "Nobody Builds a Cigar Box Guitar Because They Want to Play Nice Things"

You simply don't go down this road because you want to play another Fender® Strat. That music has been spun a million times over. This is a deeper quest.

If you're you looking for a modern method of crafting a perfect guitar from a cigar box for playing fancy music, then you can stop right here. This is something different. This book is a quest for deeper music . . . deeper living. Deep.

For me, the story starts in 1993 at a period when the blues first hit me like a ton of bricks. As an amateur musician, hearing this music caused me to abandon thrash metal and punk for this older American art form. I think it was Jimi Hendrix's "Red House" that started it for me. From there, I had to learn more about this music.

I started digging for more information. If Jimi Hendrix was so good, then who came before him? I unearthed Muddy Waters braggadocio hollers, Hound Dog Taylor's gnarled slide, and Howlin' Wolf's howl. I kept on digging. Soon, I fell into a pit of the deep stuff . . . the Delta Blues of the 1920s and 30s. Blind Willie Johnson's hellfire and damnation preaching, Mississippi John Hurt's murder ballads sung with a smile, and Cryin' Sam Collins' sorrowful and out-of-tune "git-fiddle" guitar.

My apartment became filled with overdue Smithsonian Folkway records from the library. I had a cheap acoustic guitar and a ¾" (2 cm) socket guitar slide beside my bed that I would use to choke old blues songs I heard on the turntable. It was a constant struggle with my fingers cramping up after hours of playing.

The blues are dangerous and I wanted to dance with it. But I kept failing. That's when I asked myself, what came before the Delta Blues? What was *one step deeper*?

At some point, I came across an interview with rockabilly legend Carl Perkins in which he described the very first guitar he owned:

*"Before I went to school, I started fooling around on a guitar. My daddy made me one with a cigar box, a broomstick, and two strands of baling wire, and I'd sit and beat on that thing."* – Carl Perkins

It was a poor man's guitar, built because he couldn't afford a store-bought acoustic. In my imagination, it was the whining sound of desperation.

It was *one step deeper*.

I had to make my own just to see if this was the Holy Grail that I was searching for in my quest.

On July 4, 1993, I built my very first cigar box guitar. These photos (see page 10) are of the actual guitar. It was built from a plank of wood from my father's barn, a cardboard Swisher Sweets box, three guitar tuners from a broken guitar, and three used guitar strings.

Perkins said his guitar had two strings, so I decided to make mine fancy and add a *third* string. When I strung it up, I immediately was able to play Sylvester Weaver's blues classic "Guitar Rag," a song that had earlier been the bane of my existence on my six-string acoustic. The three strings played with a slide made perfect sense to me, and the songs kept pouring out of the box.

I had found my instrument.

A cigar box guitar, in its most primal form, is broken to begin with. It shouldn't work,

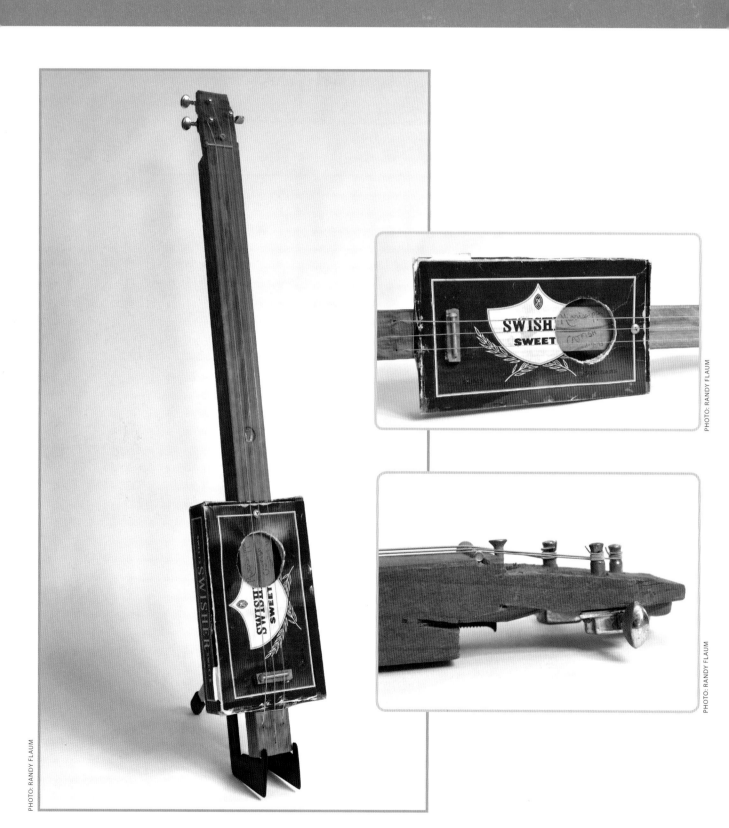

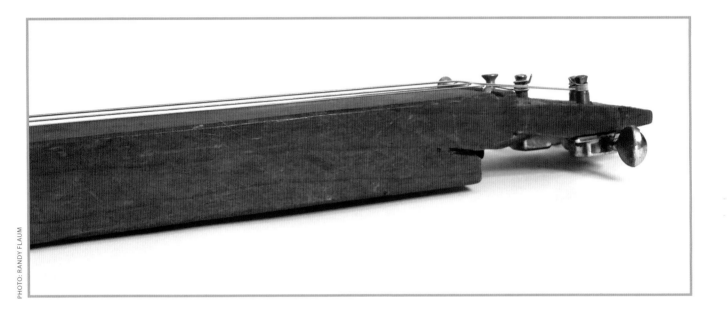

PHOTO: RANDY FLAUM

but it still does. The sounds are otherworldly, like stepping inside the grooves of an old Victrola record. The box itself was crafted by manufacturers simply to hold 25 cigars, look enticing on a store counter, and carry a tax stamp. No thought was ever given to whether it would be acoustically tuned for performance.

And yet it has the exact sound and spirit I was looking for.

It's been 25 years since I built that first cigar box guitar, and since then I've only slightly refined the style of that very first one. In the thousands of instruments I've built since that first one, I experimented with adding frets, pickups, and other elements. The further I would push the idea, the more the muse would pull me back to the simple three-string slide style of the original Swisher Sweets guitar.

This not a gimmick guitar. It's not about some educated egghead guitarist making cheeky viral videos while "slumming it" on a homemade cigar box guitar. It's digging deep

A decade ago, I "retired" the Swisher Sweets cigar box guitar by hanging it at Unkl Ray's Bar in Hinton, WV. Unfortunately, the iconic roadhouse closed several years later, but owner Ray Nutter kept my guitar preserved and in perfect condition. It was only after I started writing this book that I asked for its return. Within two days of my message to Ray, it was delivered to my front porch. Thanks, Ray. You're the true Washboard Wizard. Let's do a Jug Fusion reunion someday.

into the past to find the music that connects with your soul and then developing your own sound from it.

Let's start digging.

## Guitarcheology: "The Horse's Bridle" Two-String Guitar, Circa 1900

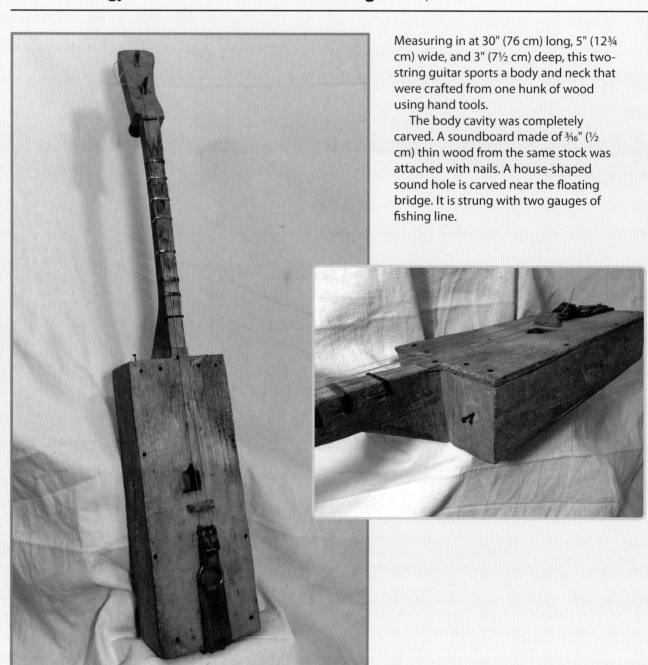

Measuring in at 30" (76 cm) long, 5" (12¾ cm) wide, and 3" (7½ cm) deep, this two-string guitar sports a body and neck that were crafted from one hunk of wood using hand tools.

The body cavity was completely carved. A soundboard made of ³⁄₁₆" (½ cm) thin wood from the same stock was attached with nails. A house-shaped sound hole is carved near the floating bridge. It is strung with two gauges of fishing line.

The angled headstock has two hand-carved tuning pegs which still work great. The frets are small pieces of nickel and copper that have been hammered over the sides and positioned at an approximated *do re mi* scale, similar to a diatonic dulcimer fretboard.

To get a better idea on the frets, I called up Derick Kemper, my current harmonica player who is also a professional blacksmith. He took one look at the guitar and said, "The frets are definitely hand hammered of some kind, but the tailpiece that holds the strings is an actual horse's bridle. I know because I just got back from shoeing horses!"

Take note at the wear marks on the face of the guitar. This instrument has been played . . . and played *hard*. Whoever built this definitely made the instrument they were searching for. The neck contains sweat marks and wear.

The guitar was discovered somewhere in New England. Amazingly, it is still very much playable.

## 1886 Newspaper Article: A Juvenile Sits on a Beer Keg and Gathers a Crowd

### A CIGAR-BOX BANJO.

**A Home-Made Instrument, and How It May Be Manufactured.**

A cigar-box banjo is something which most boys have heard of, and some have attempted, with more or less success, to make. Possibly their older relatives have ridiculed the home made instrument, and it has had to contend against prejudice, which, as we know, is almost fatal to success. Nevertheless such a banjo, if carefully made and properly strung, can be made to give forth very musical tones, and where the "real thing" can not be had the combination of cigar-box and broomstick makes a good substitute. If you would like to try your hands at it, I will tell you how to go to work.

Procure a cigar box eight and a quarter inches long, four and three quarter inches wide, and a quarter inches deep. This is the ordinary size of a box used to contain fifty cigars.

The bottom of the box forms the head of the banjo, thus allowing the cover to be opened or shut. In each end of the box cut two round holes, three quarters of an inch in diameter, half an inch from the top and an equal distance from the two sides of the box.

With a lead pencil mark off, on a piece of soft wood nineteen inches long, four inches wide, and half an inch thick, the shape of the handle, as shown in Fig 2. Before sawing the handle out, the four key holes should be bored, each hole being a quarter of an inch in diameter. Then shape the handle according to the outline of the diagram, and across the top of the handle cut a groove three-sixteenths of an inch wide and equally deep (A, Fig 1); this is to hold a small bridge to keep the strings from touching the handle.

In the side of the handle drill a hole half an inch above the angle (B, Fig 1)—this is to hold the fifth key; and just below the angle a groove three sixteenths of an inch wide and equally deep should be cut out for the purpose of holding a small bridge for the fifth string (C, Fig 1).

From an old broom cut a piece of stick twenty four inches long, whittle this flat on one side, and on the other side, eight inches from the end, cut the stick away so that it will slope and become flat at the end (Fig 2). Eight and three quarter inches at the other end of the stick must be cut away, so as to fit snugly the holes in the cigar box, the end projecting slightly. This broomstick Fig. 2 is the backbone of the handle, which is fastened to it by two three quarter inch screws as shown in Fig 3.

Five keys shaped like Fig 4 can be cut out of tough pieces of wood, each piece being half an inch thick, two and a quarter inches long, and one inch wide. Make those belonging to the key board fit tightly in their holes. The key for the fifth string can be cut half an inch shorter than the others. Each key should have a hole bored through it, as shown in Fig 4.

The small bridge is a piece of wood a quarter of an inch high and three sixteenths of an inch wide, which is made to fit the groove (Fig 1, A), with four notches cut in to conduct the strings. A similar bridge with only one notch and a quarter of an inch long will answer for the fifth string.

The large bridge is made of a piece of wood two inches long, five eighths of an inch wide, and a quarter o' an inch thick. The shape of the bridge can be seen in the illustration of the finished banjo. Five notches an equal distance from each other should then be cut in the top edge of the bridge.

The tail piece is the piece to which the strings are attached at the lower end of the instrument. It is made from a piece of hard wood an inch and a half long, an inch and a quarter wide and a quarter of an inch thick. Five small holes an equal distance apart and a quarter of an inch from the end of the piece of wood must first be drilled, and through the small end two holes a quarter of an inch apart and three eighths of an inch from the end should be drilled to allow a piece of wire about six inches in length to pass through them. A piece of tin an inch and a quarter long and three-quarters of an inch wide, bent so as to fit on the edge of the box, will be required. Strings can be purchased at almost any music store.

Having purchased the strings, begin to put the various parts together by fitting the handle through the holes in the cigar box and the small bridges in their respective grooves. The tail piece is then fastened close to the end of the box by twisting the wire around the projecting piece of broomstick and staying it. Place the piece of bent tin on the edge of the box, under the wire holding the tail-piece, thus preventing the wire from damaging the box. Fit the keys in the key-board and the short key into the hole in the side of the handle. Knot the strings before threading them through the holes in the tail-piece. Before tightening the strings the last bridge is placed under the strings, two and a half inches from the end of the box, and your banjo is finished. —*John Richards, in Harper's Young People.*

*Historic cigar box banjo plans, first published in 1886.*

## St. Joseph Herald.

VOL. XXVI.      ST. JOSEPH, BERRIEN COUNTY, MICHIGAN, SATURDAY, MARCH 20, 1886.      NO. 47.

*GALVESTON (TX) DAILY NEWS*, **THURSDAY, APRIL 15, 1886**

Perched upon a lager beer keg in an obscure locality in the city, sat a diminutive musician yesterday. His legs were crossed, his lips were moving, and his hands were playing a [homemade] guitar. This instrument was rudely but cleverly fashioned, and exhibited traces of an inventive genius in its maker.

A [cigar box] of the usual size constituted the body, and the handle was composed of a piece of lath about [8"; 20⅓ cm] in length, over which strings of tightly-drawn India rubber were laid, and caught at the end on roughly-made keys. The box was completely enclosed, with the exception of a round hole in the center for a [sounding board].

Altogether, it was an original instrument, and though crudely constructed, was capable of emitting melodious strains. Considering the imperfections of it in the comparison with a genuine guitar, the player handled the strings very deftly.

When seen, he was earnestly playing a tune, and no one appeared to enjoy it more than himself, though the barkeeper whose keg he was sitting upon came out and shaded his eyes on the curious object. The selection was an old-time melody, and he soon had a crowd of sympathizers around him. While playing, his different antics and motions were peculiar and amusing. His lips went in and out, keeping perfect time to the music. He swayed himself from side to side, shut one eye, then the other, then rolled both up until only the whites were visible, apparently in a perfect delirium of enjoyment.

In the midst of all this a great catastrophe occurred. The strings all snapped but one. But to the wonder of those present he continued to draw music out of his one string. As he finished and crawled down from his perch, he was variously interrogated, but jumping into a small wagon hitched to a good-sized goat, he rapidly made off amid the shouts of the crowd and uproarious laughter.

It was evident that he did not wish to be bothered and had his goat handy for any disagreeable emergency.

# CHAPTER 2: How to Build a Three-String Cigar Box Guitar

"The Old Macanudo" cigar box guitar is not just another cigar box guitar.

Within a year of building that Swisher Sweets cigar box guitar, I discovered 1" x 2" x 3' (25 x 50 x 914 mm) poplar wood stashed in the craft wood section of a Home Depot. Unlike the big hunk of barn wood I used on the original neck, these sticks of poplar worked just as well for guitar necks and were more readily available than the barn wood.

I also discovered that cigar companies had returned to using solid wood or plywood for their cigar boxes. These provided an even louder tone than the cardboard box of my original axe. I would haunt the local cigar stores, begging for any empty boxes lying around.

In 1996, I built a handful of cigar box guitars to sell at a local street fair. I realized at the time that, with the exception of my Swisher Sweets guitar (which was not so loud in a crowd setting), I had given away or sold any previous cigar box guitars I had built. I needed to select one from the current batch to be my main

Performing on a bale of hay at a street festival in 1996 with my glorious mullet. The Macanudo cigar box guitar was brand new, without a single scratch on it. (That would soon change.)

PHOTO: RANDY FLAUM

Another view of the Macanudo cigar box guitar, taken on the day it was made.

performer for that fest, so I strummed them all, listening for the loudest one. The winner was made from a Macanudo Portofino Café box.

I played that guitar at the festival and onward for the next two decades!

This beat-up guitar has appeared on every one of my albums, been used in hundreds of gigs, and is still playable. I'm slowly wearing a hole in the plywood top and the neck is caked with grime, blood,

and sweat. Autographs of performers who shared the stage grace the instrument. (Famous signatures include The Drifters, The Presidents of the United States of America, fingerstyle blues master Rory Block, and gospel blues legend Glenn Kaiser.)

Because the old Macanudo has been the perfect muse for all these years, it has become the template for these plans. (How I wish I could see your face when the first string rings out as you tune up!)

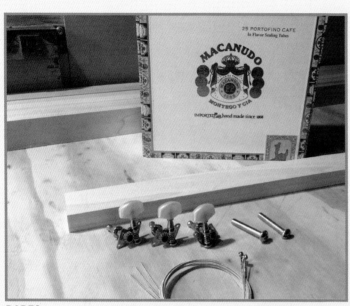

## PARTS

- 1" x 2" x 32" (2½ x 5 x 81 cm) piece of poplar wood (available from the craft wood section of most big box hardware stores)
- Three guitar tuners*
- Two machine screws, size ¼" (⅔ cm) – 20 x 1½" (3¾ cm)
- Eight small ⅜" (1 cm) guitar tuner screws
- Three #8 x ½" (1¼ cm) round head screws
- Three guitar strings: Choose A, D, G strings from a pack of conventional acoustic guitar strings
- Cigar box with a drop-in lid

## TOOLS

- Pencil
- Ruler
- Carpenter's square
- Miter gauge
- Table saw
- Scroll saw or coping saw
- Rotary tool with a ¼" (⅔ cm) straight bit or a file
- Woodburning pen with chisel tip (optional)
- Sandpaper: 80 grit and 220 grit
- Carpenter's knife
- Drill
- Drill bits: 1/16" (1½ mm) and 5/16" (¾ cm)
- Hacksaw or belt sander
- Phillips screwdriver (#1)
- Gloss polyurethane

*Note: The measurements in these plans utilize open gear guitar tuners with 5/16" (¾ cm) diameter tuner bushings.

## Choosing a Box: Boite Nature vs. Drop-In Lid

The two most common wooden cigar box styles are "Boite Nature," which features a lid that overlaps the sides, and "drop-in lid," which has a flat panel lid that fits within the sides of the box. Although cigar box guitars can be made from just about any box, I prefer drop-in lid boxes for their simplicity. These plans are tailored to this style box. Drop-ins only take a few cuts of a coping saw to prep for guitar building, shortening the process.

My personal favorite cigar box is the Macanudo Portofino Café box, which has great acoustic volume and tone.

Building tip: An 8-foot (244 cm) length of 1" x 2" (25 x 50 mm) poplar will yield three guitar necks when cut at 32" (81 cm) lengths. This may not be relevant as you build your first cigar box guitar, but soon you'll discover that once you build one and hear those strings ring out, you'll become addicted to building and will start envisioning many more! Get the eight-foot (244 cm) plank. Trust me.

Figure 2-1.

Figure 2-2.

Figure 2-3.

Figure 2-4.

Figure 2-5.

### Checking for Bow in the Wood

Pick up the 32" (81 cm) section of poplar and look down the edge like you were lining up the sights of a shotgun (Figure 2-1). If the wood has a bow in it, make a pencil mark on the side with the top of the arch as seen in the illustration. The convex arch side will be the fretboard and the string tension will help to counteract the bowing. If the wood is straight, then skip this step.

### Planning Out the Neck

In keeping with the old tradition, the cigar box guitar neck will go through the cigar box and emerge out the back, serving as both the fretboard *and* internal bracing. The neck's job is to do all the work, allowing the box to vibrate and sing freely.

The neck will need to be notched out to fit the lid of the cigar box (Figure 2-2), as well as an area for the headstock. You'll need a pencil, ruler, and carpenter's square.

From left to right, mark the following points on the neck (Figure 2-3):

- 1" (2½ cm) butt end
- 4¼" (10¾ cm) bridge location
- 27¼" (69¼ cm) nut location
- 27¾" (70½ cm) headstock curve
- 28" (71 cm) headstock notching area

Remove the lid from the cigar box by gently cutting the paper hinge with a sharp knife (Figure 2-4).

Place the cigar box lid against the 1" (2½ cm) mark of the neck (Figure 2-5). Mark a line at the opposite end of the box lid; this is the neck joint area.

Figure 2-6.

Figure 2-7.

Figure 2-8.

## Notching the Headstock and Body Route

Cigar box guitar builders of the past would use pocketknives or handsaws to remove the wood. Many people use coping saws or bandsaws. After decades of building them, I've found the best way to make nice, tight fits is to use multiple swipes from a table saw. This method will help control the depth of each cut, ensuring a tight fit and allowing the box lid to have minimal contact with the neck.

Table saw prep:

- Set the table saw blade to ⅛" (⅓ cm) high.
- Set the miter gauge for 90 degrees square
- Check all safety covers

Use a carpenter's square to gauge the depth (Figure 2-6). Place the neck facedown on the table saw. Starting at the 28" (71 cm) mark (Headstock Notching Area) *carefully* cut notches from the 28" (71 cm) mark to the end (Figure 2-7), using the miter gauge as your guide for perfect 90-degree lines.

Go slowly and be consistent. Make sure you are pressing down on the neck as you make the swipes, ensuring that even bowed wood gets the proper notching (Figure 2-8). Remove all the wood from the headstock area.

*"On Saturdays, barbers sat their customers in the shade on the porch of the Store, and troubadours on their ceaseless crawlings through the South leaned on its benches and sang their sad songs of The Brazos while they played juice harps and cigar-box guitars."*

**FROM *I KNOW WHY THE CAGED BIRD SINGS* BY MAYA ANGELOU**

Figure 2-9.

Figure 2-10.

## Notching the Body Area

The empty wooden box is the resonator, or "broadcaster," as vagrant musician Eddie "One String" Jones would describe it. It's the element that *sings* in a cigar box guitar. The lid must have the freedom to vibrate and amplify the strings in the most acoustic way possible. The goal is to attach the neck to the box in a way that allows solid bracing, *but minimal contact* with the box lid.

The table saw will be used to notch the body route just like the headstock. However, we will use a two-tiered notch, allowing the box lid to only touch the neck at the beginning of the box, in the middle where the bridge rests, and at the very end. The rest of the neck will have a slightly deeper notch to keep it from touching the underside of the lid.

Place the detached cigar box lid flat on the table saw, butted up against the blade. Raise the blade to the exact height of the box's thickness (Figure 2-9).

1. Cut a notch at the 1" (2½ cm) mark, making sure to position the blade to the right of the pencil line. (You don't want to cut the notch in the center of the line). Make two swipes to give you about a ¼" (⅔ cm) notch.
2. Cut three notches at the 4¼" (10¾ cm) line (bridge), one notch on each side of the pencil line, and one in the center, giving about a ½" (1¼ cm) notch area.
3. Cut a notch at the box endpoint (Neck Joint Area) on the left side of the pencil line.

Completed notches should be as shown in Figure 2-10. Raise the blade up about ⅛" (⅓ cm). Notch out all areas in between the ends and the bridge as shown in Figure 2-11.

Figure 2-11.

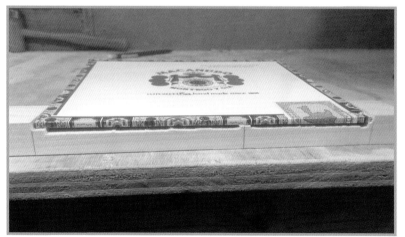

Figure 2-12.

## Two Blues Legends and a Homemade Guitar: Robert Johnson, Robert Lockwood Jr., and the Phonograph Guitar

**EXCERPTED FROM *GUITAR PLAYER* MAGAZINE, JULY 1991**

One day when Robert Johnson was taking a break from his roaming, he sat down to make a guitar with his young pupil Robert Lockwood, Jr. What they made wasn't a diddley bow, the one-string instrument many fledgling bluesmen built by streching a piece of wire between two nails. Johnson and Lockwood were intent on building something more sophisticated. Johnson shaped the wood and then made the body from a phonograph. Lockwood, who had been happily strumming away on Johnson's Stella, used the guitar for just over a year before it began to tear apart because [Lockwood says], "We couldn't get the right type of glue."

When complete, you should be able to fit the cigar box lid snugly inside the neck pocket (Figure 2-12). Turn it on the side and make sure only the ends and bridge section touch the underside of the lid.

Figure 2-13.

Figure 2-14. Place a piece of scrap wood under the neck to prevent drill bit blowout of the wood.

Figure 2-15.

Figure 2-16.

Figure 2-17.

## Tuner Drilling and Headstock Prep

Mark the tuner holes on the headstock between ⅜" (1 cm) and ½" (1¼ cm) from the edge of the wood (Figure 2-13) to ensure your tuner buttons have clearance from the wood when installed. The holes should also be spaced at least 1" (2½ cm) away from each other so rear mounting plates don't overlap on the back. Drill the holes using a ⁵⁄₁₆" (¾ cm) drill bit (Figure 2-14).

Draw a ¼" (⅔ cm) circle (Figure 2-15) to round the headstock notch. Using a scroll saw, coping saw, or rotary tool, remove the wood, carefully blending it to the face of the headstock.

**Grooving the nut slot:** Using a square, draw a line across the fretboard at the "Nut" mark (Figure 2-16). Carve a groove across the line using a rotary tool with a ¼" (⅔ cm) straight bit or a file (Figure 2-17). A depth of ⅛" (⅓ cm) deep is recommended. Make sure the slot is just wide enough to fit the machine screw.

Figure 2-18.

### String Anchor Holes

Go to the other end of the neck and mark three string anchor holes, each ⁷⁄₁₆" (11 mm) apart from each other. These holes will anchor the ball end of the strings. Make sure the holes are at least ½" (1¼ cm) from the end of the stick. Use a ¹⁄₁₆" (1½ mm) bit and drill straight (Figure 2-18).

### Sanding

Using 80-grit sandpaper, smooth the face of the headstock. Progress to 220-grit and sand the entire neck. Round the edges of the neck as you sand.

### Shaping the Neck (and Inhaling the Mojo)

There's nothing like a cigar box guitar in your hands, especially one you made yourself. I've played hundreds of stages with mine and the neck is now covered in sweat, grime, scratches, and even blood. The neck feels like an extension of my own hands.

As you're sanding the neck of the instrument you're building, hold it in your hand. This is going to be *your* guitar. How's that neck feel in your hand? A little sharp? Smooth those corners a little more. Take your time with the 220-grit sandpaper and finish it right. You're not making a piece of furniture; you're making a living, breathing instrument capable of expressing your innermost emotions. This machine will sing.

I cannot stress enough the importance of listening to good music as you build. What songs do you want to play on your cigar box guitar? Deep Delta blues? Old time Appalachian? *Play those songs through your stereo* as you build, and your hands will unconsciously shape and mold the guitar toward those sounds.

## Scale Length and Woodburning Fret Lines

When I first started marking the fret lines on my instruments back in 1994, I would lay the neck blank beside my old Stella acoustic guitar that had a 23" (58½ cm) neck and copy the fret lines. After more than two decades, I still use that scale. It works fine and causes less tension than a 24" (61 cm) or 25" (63½ cm) scale, which means the neck won't bow as easily over time.

### MARKING FRET LINES

*Note: If you have sanded off the line for the nut, take a ruler and measure 23" (58½ cm) from the bridge mark and re-mark a line for the nut.*

Go to page 173 and line up the 23" (58½ cm) fret template from the nut line. Mark the frets according to the template and then use a carpenter's square to draw the lines straight across with a pencil. You can also mark fret dots as shown on the template.

I also add side fret dots to my cigar box guitars because it helps the player gauge where the fret lines are located. I simply mark a small dot on the side (Figure 2-19), left side of the neck for right-handed guitars, right side of the neck for southpaws.

When I was first building cigar box guitars in the mid-1990s, I wore out several blues cassettes from overplay. Most of the titles were from Columbia Records' "Roots and Blues" series, including the albums, *Blind Willie Johnson: The Complete Recordings*, the compilation of slide blues, *The Slide Guitar: Bottles, Knives & Steel*, and the jug band compilation *Good Time Blues: Kazoos, Washboards and Cowbells*. The songs contained in those three cassettes still return to my concert set lists after all these years. They've become a part of me.

When I would finally finish a guitar and tune it up, I invariably gravitated toward a song I was listening to and would find a way to play it on the instrument I just built.

*Take your time on that neck.* Get it shaped to your hand so that it can talk for you. Listen to music. Soon, you'll be playing songs on this machine. Inhale some of the mojo as it mixes with the sawdust.

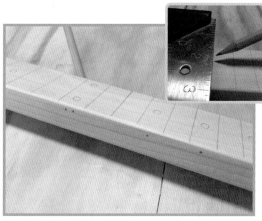

Figure 2-19.

Figure 2-20.

### WOODBURNING FRET LINES

Use a wedge or chisel-shaped woodburning tip to draw lines for frets. Let that iron heat up fully and then use a steady hand to trace the lines. Don't press down hard, let the heat of the pen do the work. Practice on scrap wood first if you're new to using a woodburning pen. Do your best to keep the lines straight and try not to stop and start again on the same line.

If your woodburning pen has a pencil tip, use it to draw the fret dots and side dots. If not, your chisel tip should suffice. Just take your time with it.

*Important! Sign your work!* You're making a piece of art and it should wear your signature with pride. Use a pencil and autograph the headstock or back of the neck with your very best signature. Add a date, too. Then take your hot woodburning pen over the signature to make it permanent (Figure 2-20).

## Applying Wood Finish to the Neck

I prefer a single coat of gloss polyurethane to the neck, but you can give yours several coats if you want a shiny coat. My original Macanudo cigar box guitar had a light coat applied to it in 1996, which started to show cool wear marks and aging soon after I started playing it.

Follow the instructions on the can. Once the finish is dry, smooth it out with steel wool. Make sure the back of that neck melts into your hand.

Fingerprints in the finish: A telltale sign of a rabid cigar box guitarist who just couldn't wait for the polyurethane to dry before stringing it up.

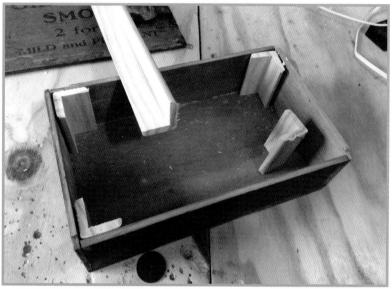

Figure 2-21.

## Preparing the Cigar Box

Strengthening the inside box corners: Cigar boxes are made using the cheapest materials with the intention of simply selling the cigars inside. No cigar manufacturer has ever commissioned cigar boxes in hopes that they would create music. With that in mind, you may need to create simple bracing inside the cigar box to hold it together a little better.

Get scrap 1" x 1" (2½ x 2½ cm) corner molding and cut it to fit the inside corners (Figure 2-21). Make sure it is cut short enough for the lid to fit inside the box. Use wood glue or a hot glue gun to affix them to the sides. Make sure you glue the bottom, as well. In paper-covered boxes, I also run a hot glue gun along the inside edges to strengthen the box.

Figure 2-22.

Figure 2-23.

Figure 2-24.

Figure 2-25.

## Creating the Neck Slots in the Box

Cut a 2" (5 cm) scrap of 1" x 2" (2½ x 5cm) wood. Find the ¾" (2 cm) center point on the scrap and mark a vertical line. Continue the line over the top side of the scrap (Figure 2-22).

Place the cigar box face down. Find the center on the sides. Mark a horizontal line with a pencil (Figure 2-23). Match line to line and trace around the scrap. Repeat on the opposite side (Figure 2-24). Using a coping saw, cut out the notch (Figure 2-25). Clean up the edges with sandpaper or a file.

There's nothing like the smell of cigar box sawdust. The scents of wood and tobacco are heavenly.

Figure 2-26.

Figure 2-27.

## Designing and Cutting Sound Holes

I love sound holes.

There's a whole scientific explanation of sound holes called Helmholtz Resonance, but let's keep that for the corporations who are mass-producing acoustic guitars in China. All we need to know is that sound holes enhance the radiation of sound by allowing air to vibrate inside the box as well as near its opening.

In all honesty, all you truly need is a small circle about the size of a quarter, cut on the lower right corner of the box lid. Anything more than that is just being fancy. I don't care . . . I love to get artistic with sound holes.

If there is one area in your cigar box guitar that allows your full artistic ability to

shine, it's in the sound holes. If you have a scroll saw in your shop, this part will get you excited.

How to plan and cut your sound holes:

The neck of your cigar box guitar will go through the box. The blue tape on the box lid shows where the neck will go (Figure 2-26). It's usually a good idea to place your sound holes away from the neck, so you don't see the wood inside, as shown in the photo.

For shapes and ideas, do an Internet image search for "guitar sound hole template." Once you print out the shape (or draw one yourself), create a stencil by tracing it on card stock and cut it out with a hobby knife (Figure 2-27).

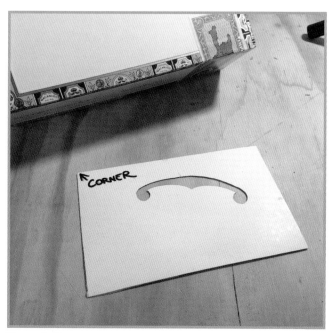

Figure 2-28.

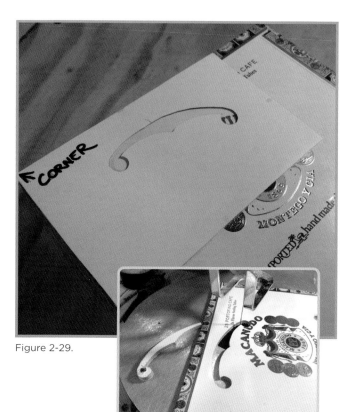

Figure 2-29.

Figure 2-30.

Determine the placement on the box and trace with a pencil (Figure 2-28). My stencil is set up to be mirrored. I simply line up the corner of the stencil with the corner of the box, trace, and then flip and repeat.

Drill pilot holes for your scroll saw or coping saw blade and then carefully cut the sound holes out (Figure 2-29).

If you're using a paper-covered box, you may need to de-burr the underside of the box lid with scrap sandpaper (Figure 2-30) in order to remove tiny bits of torn paper.

## Install the Tuners

At the headstock, gently tap in the bushings for the guitar tuners (Figure 2-31). Turn the headstock over and install the tuners (Figure 2-32). As you are positioning them, make sure the brass gears are pointed *toward* the body of the guitar. (Placing the tuner backward eventually causes the string tension to pull the shaft away from the gear, stripping it out over time.)

Figure 2-31.

Figure 2-32.

## Install the Tuners (continued)

Figure 2-33.

Figure 2-34.

Figure 2-35.

Mark the screw holes with a pencil and drill pilot holes using a ¹⁄₁₆" (1½ mm) bit. Then screw in the tuners using a small-tip #1 Phillips screwdriver (Figure 2-33).

Both the neck and the box are now complete and ready to be joined together. Notice how the two fit together like puzzle pieces. The neck goes through the box and the lid covers the top, fitting into the neck notch (Figure 2-34).

You can choose to glue the box lid to the body, use tiny screws (such as these ³⁄₈" [1 cm] screws made for guitar tuners), or both. Personally, I glue the lid down with a hot glue gun and then use the screws to make sure everything stays in place (Figure 2-35).

Figure 2-36.

Using screws, secure the neck to the box lid on both sides with one screw (Figure 2-36). This will keep the neck from moving around as you play, ensuring better tuning.

Take one of the machine screws and cut off the side of the head, as shown in Figure 2-37. Use either a hacksaw or simply grind it down on a belt sander. This will serve as the bridge for the strings. The other machine screw stays intact. You'll need this cut bolt once the guitar gets strung up.

Figure 2-37.

## Bluesman Albert Collins, His Cigar Box Guitar, and His Rattlesnake Secret

**EXCERPTED FROM A *GUITAR PLAYER* MAGAZINE INTERVIEW, JULY 1993**

*Interviewer: You made your first guitar out of a . . .*

**Albert Collins:** Cigar box. People back in them days couldn't afford no guitar, man. I took a hay-baling wire, and it was rough, man! You couldn't do nothing with it, so I just be banging it! [Laughs.]

*I: When you were a child, you reportedly put rattlesnake rattles inside your guitar.*

**A.C.:** Mm-hmm. Some other people used to take pennies and put them in their hollow box. It gets a good sound. The rattlesnake rattles—you dry 'em out and put 'em in. Lightnin' Hopkins taught me that trick.

*I: Would you shake the guitar while you're playing?*

**A.C:** Nah, you just put 'em in . . . You take about four or five of those rattlers, dry 'em out, and put them inside your hollow box guitar . . .

*I: What's the theory behind this?*

**A.C.:** I don't know. A lot of people did it around before my time, and I started doing it. . . I guess it's because the rattlers inside makes a weird sound.

*I: [Collins also discussed a second homemade guitar that came after the first cigar box guitar] Is this the guitar someone made for you out of an oak tree?*

**A.C.:** Yeah, that guy used to play with Ernest Tubbs—he was a country western singer . . . I used to drive a truck for him. He said, "I'm gonna make you a guitar." I said okay, and it was so big, I couldn't hardly get my hand around it. [Laughs.]

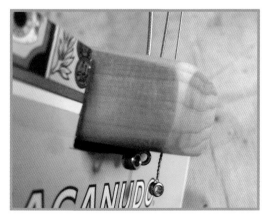

Figure 2-38.

### Stringing and Setup

The strings run through the butt end of the instrument (Figure 2-38). Feed them through the back, making sure to pull them through until the ball end touches the underside of the butt. Use the A string as the low string, located toward the upper bout of the guitar. The middle is the D guitar string and the high string is G.

After attaching the strings to the tuners, tighten them up just enough to keep them from being wobbly. Insert the uncut machine screw into the nut slot (Figure 2-39).

Figure 2-39.

Figure 2-40.

Measure exactly 23" (58½ cm) from the nut and put a mark on the cigar box (Figure 2-40). This is the bridge location. Insert the cut machine screw at the mark under the strings. The string tension holds the bolt in place. No glue is needed.

Because of the headstock angle, the strings will require retainers to hold them down behind the nut. If not, they will not properly set on the nut. Space the strings ⅜" (1 cm) apart at the nut and hold them in place with one hand (Figure 2-41).

Take notice to the angle of the strings to the tuner. Mark and drill ¹⁄₁₆" (1½ mm) pilot holes beside each string on the inside of the angle break for each. Insert a #8 x ½" (1¼ cm) round head screw in each hole and screw each one down just until the string holds tension behind the nut. The head of the screw becomes a retainer for the string (Figure 2-42).

Be prepared for the most magical step of all: tuning the guitar up and hearing loud, distinct tones emanating from the box. There's no feeling like it in the world. This empty wooden box was made to hold hand-rolled cigars, but now it's singing on its own.

Figure 2-41.

Figure 2-42.

### Setting Up, Choosing a Slide Playing Your Cigar Box Guitar

This is the instrument of the American peasant. Kids played 'em. New Orleans spasm bands played 'em. The cigar box guitar is the instrument for somebody who's "got the boogie in him . . . and it gotta come out!" Don't over-think this stuff.

You have three strings tuned to a chord and you use a slide to fret other chords up the neck. This is an instrument to *play by ear*. Grab a guitar tuner (they even make tuner apps for your phone) or sit at the piano and plink out the notes. Let's tune this sucker!

Start by tuning your guitar to Open G (G, D, G). If you're using a piano, the low G is the same as the G located two octaves below middle C on the keyboard. The middle string is tuned to D and the high string is also a G, tuned one octave higher than the

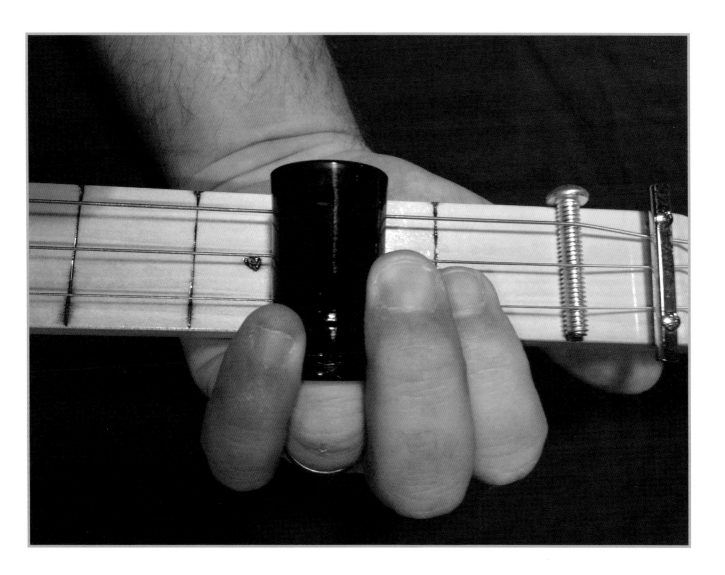

low string. GDG: a simple power chord that has a universe of possibilities on your cigar box guitar.

So now you'll need a slide. In the Depression Era, bluesmen would break a bottle on the sidewalk and grind the bottleneck down to a playable nub. My first slide was a ¾" (2 cm) Craftsman socket. Whatever you choose, your slide needs to be comfortable on your finger of choice.

Guitar slides can be found objects such as sockets, glass medicine bottles, a section of copper pipe, or even a closed pocketknife. There are also hundreds of handcrafted and factory-made guitar slides. Personally, I prefer shorter guitar slides that give my finger the mobility to race around the three strings. My slide collection has grown to more than 100 slides, and I've curated some of the best styles in my little store, *www.StubbySlide.com*.

### Guide to Three-String Cigar Box Guitar Tunings: All tunings listed low to high

**Open A:** A, E, A (one octave higher)
**Open G:** G, D, G (one octave higher)
**A7** (the magic jazz tuning): A, E, G
**A6** (Hawaiian tuning): A, E, F#
**G9** (mandolin-style tuning): G, D, A
**Dirty E:** E, E (one octave higher), B

I have filmed a full video series on How to Play Cigar Box Guitar. These short and easy lessons are at *www.PoorMansGuitar.com*, free to watch without any subscription. Before wrestling with music notations or other resources, watch the videos. It's the simple, "Here, lemme show you"-style of lessons that will get you playing fast. *I want you to play your cigar box guitar.* Building them is fun, but playing them is magical.

Holding the slide: As you can see, I keep my slide on the top two knuckles of my finger. This allows my hand to be

## DIY Guitar Slides of Blues Legends

• **Blind Willie Johnson's** father made him a one-string cigar box guitar when he was only five years old. Johnson learned to play melodies up and down the string using a pocketknife as a slide. When he finally got a conventional guitar in his teens, he transferred that playing style over, playing melodies up and down the high E string while the other strings rang out.

• **Elmore James** used a thin metal vacuum tube cover from a radio.

• **Hound Dog Taylor's** guitar slide was a 2½" (6⅓ cm) section of chrome pipe taken from a kitchen table leg. He added even more mass to it by hammering a narrower piece of pipe inside. He placed the slide on his *first* pinky. (Taylor was born with six fingers on each hand. Legend has it, his extra finger on his picking hand kept getting in his way one night at a drunken gig—Taylor pulled out a knife and cut it off!)

• **Cedell Davis'** hands were crippled from polio, but that didn't stop him from playing guitar. He simply placed a butter knife between his fingers and used it as a slide.

• **Jimi Hendrix** was known for using anything nearby as a slide, including steel beer cans. He uses his Zippo® lighter for the slide part on "All Along the Watchtower."

• **Duane Allman** was nursing a cold in 1968 when his brother, Gregg, showed up with Taj Mahal's first album and a bottle of Coricidin pills. Once Duane put the album on the turntable and heard the iconic sound of Taj's slide guitar, he dumped the Coricidin pills on the table, peeled the label off the glass pill bottle, and placed it on his finger as a slide. It was the perfect fit and became his chosen slide for the rest of his short life.

• **Johnny Winter** used one piece of conduit pipe as a slide for his entire career. Prior to discovering the perfectly fitting piece of pipe, he tried wristwatch crystals, lipstick cases, and bottles.

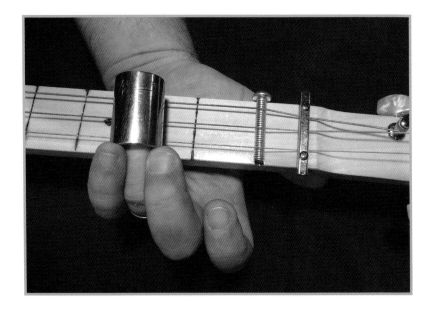

more relaxed as I play. Notice how the slide is placed *directly over* the fret line and not in between frets. You don't need to mash the strings down hard onto the fretboard; the slide does all the work. You simply have to let the slide make contact with the strings in order to change the pitch.

Now go watch those video lessons at *www.PoorMansGuitar.com*. Welcome to your new addiction.

## Guitarcheology: The Ethiopian Masenqo

A cigar box guitar is nothing more than a stick jammed through an empty box. These *neck through box* designs, also called "spike fiddle"-style instruments, can be traced back to African instruments such as the *guimbri* and *mosenqo*, which features a neck that goes through the body of the instrument.

The masenqo is a one-string fiddle from Ethiopia strung with horsehair that has been twisted tight into a string. It is played with a bow, also made from horsehair, and features an animal skin head which projects tone quite well. Masenqos are used by Ethiopian minstrels, known as *azmaris*, and are fretted by simply pressing the fingers onto the string while bowing. There is no fretboard, but the fingers act much like a guitar slide on a guitar string.

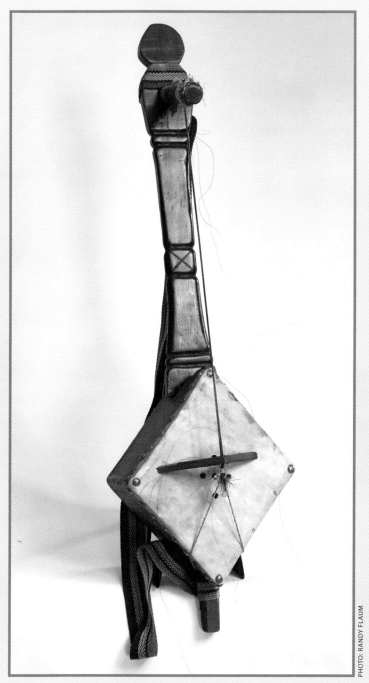

PHOTO: RANDY FLAUM

## Sound Hole Ideas

Figure 2-43.

Figure 2-44.

### Renaissance "C-Hole" Style

This simple sound hole design (see Figure 2-43) dates back to 16th century violins. It's elegant and easier to cut on a scroll saw than a more detailed F-hole. When I first started making and selling cigar box guitars back in the 1990s, I called my company Catfish Music Works. The C-shape of sound hole complemented the name. I still use this design to this day.

### Long Sound Hole with Furnace Grate

Sometimes a cigar box's style dictates the sound hole. This cigar box guitar was made with a Kuba Deluxe box that originally had a long Plexiglas® window in the top to show the cigars (see Figure 2-44). I removed the Plexiglas® and substituted it with tin furnace grate material I purchased from the hardware store. It gave the guitar a confessional booth appearance.

## Sound Hole Ideas (Continued)

Figure 2-45.

### Classic Radio-Style Holes with Sceen Wire

I wanted to give this guitar a 1930s retro look (see Figure 2-45), so I drew up a series of slotted sound holes. After creating a template, I cut them out with a scroll saw and cleaned them up with sandpaper and files. I then glued common window screen wire onto the underside with a hot glue gun. This gave it an even more convincing look.

I have also used window screen wire on other sound hole shapes. The final result is always a cleaner, more finished appearance, as seen with these traditional F-holes (see Figure 2-46).

Figure 2-46.

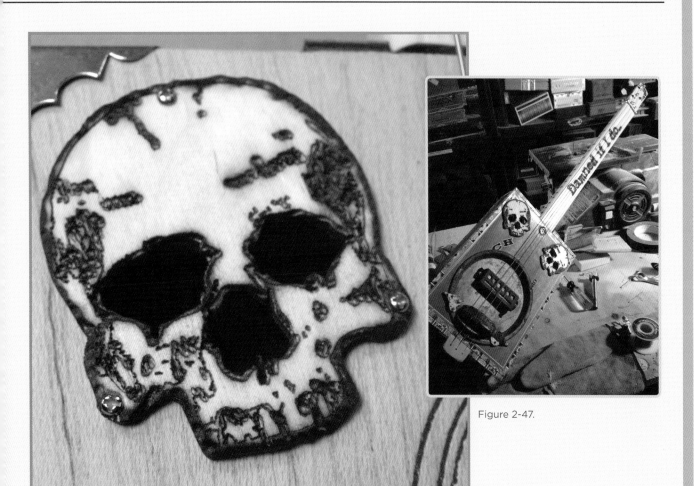

Figure 2-47.

## Skull with Sound Hole Eyes and Nose

I created this sound hole cover by drawing an old skull onto a piece of thin plywood (see Figure 2-47). I then used my scroll saw to remove the eyes and nose areas, and finished the look with my woodburning pen. The design was so successful that it was turned into an actual sound hole cover product for a cigar box guitar parts company.

## Sound Hole Ideas (Continued)

Figure 2-48.

### Beer Cap Screens

I always keep a huge box of bottle caps in my shop. (In order to save my liver, I skip the drinking part and buy used caps on eBay!) This is just one method I've used them to give a hobo look. A series of 1" (2½ cm) holes were drilled into the face of this cigar box guitar (see Figure 2-48). I then drilled holes into the bottle caps and hot glued them to the underside of the cigar box lid. Matching the red caps to the maroon trim on the box gave it a completed look.

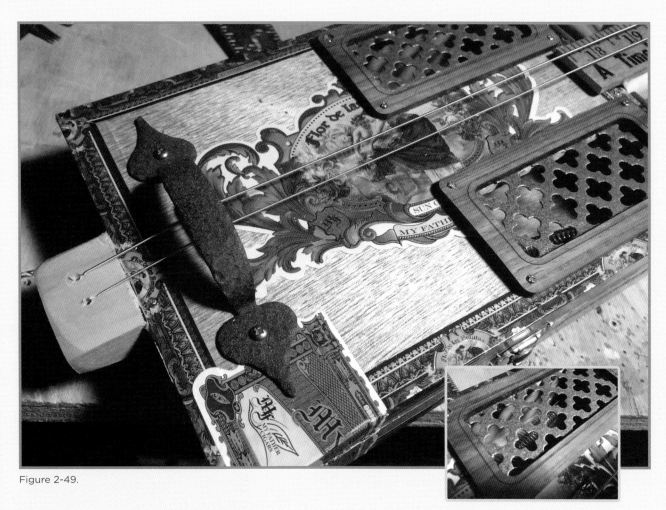

Figure 2-49.

## More Furnace Grate Sound Holes

These sound holes may be very striking visually, but they're actually simple to create
(see Figure 2-49). I started with a pair of Padauk pickup rings (originally intended
for mounting a mini humbucker pickup) and added a small section of metal lattice
I picked up at Lowes. To achieve the rust look, I painted the lattice with Rust-Oleum®
dark brown textured spray paint first and then attached them to the underside of
pickup rings with hot glue.

## Sound Hole Ideas (Continued)

### Peep-Show Sound Hole and Coin Slot

I've also used these pickup rings in a series of art cigar box guitars called "Peep Show" (see Figure 2-50). Instead of placing tin lattice, I let kept the sound holes open and placed an antique photo inside the box, giving them the look of an old dime-show girlie movie.

Figure 2-50.

Figure 2-51.

The second sound hole looks like a coin slot (see Figure 2-51). To make this, I first created the design in Photoshop and then printed it out. I had a scrap piece of thin mahogany that I cut to shape and then wood burned the art. A proper coin slot was cut on my scroll saw.

# CHAPTER 3: Variations on a Theme – Pickups and Mods to the Three-String Cigar Box Guitar

**PARTS:**
- Acoustic guitar preamp with piezo rod pickup. (The style used throughout this book was purchased at *www.GittyPreamp.com*. Similar preamps can also be found by searching "Cigar Box Guitar Preamp With Piezo Rod Pickup" on eBay or Amazon.)

**TOOLS:**
- Coping saw or rotary tool with a cutting bit
- Pliers or crescent wrench

Performing at the 1997 Rehoboth Beach Autumn Jazz Festival. Notice the tie tack microphone jammed into the sound hole. (Once again, I must point out my glorious mullet.)

In the thousand cigar box guitars I've built over the years, I've experimented with pickups, frets, and any wild DIY idea I could add to an instrument. The plans in this book provide a basic canvas for you to modify, customize, and explore, as well.

These variations include a tried-and-true pickup system that will deliver the most convincing amplified acoustic tone along with some other fun mods.

## The Best Low-Budget Acoustic Pickup for Your Cigar Box Guitar

When I first started performing live with my cigar box guitar in 1995, I would shove a tie-tack microphone into the sound hole to amplify it. It was just a cheap $20 mic from Radio Shack that was originally intended to clip on a speaker's tie or collar when giving seminars. I was nervously playing coffee shop gigs at the time and the mic was good enough for the job at hand.

Between then and now, the instrument's popularity has exploded all over the world and people have tried all types of pickups in many different setups. I've played them all and the following method is the best way I have found to deliver an amplified acoustic sound that captures the cigar box guitar's character.

This setup uses a piezo rod pickup that is sandwiched between the neck-through area and the underside of the box lid. The piezo rod is the same type of pickup found underneath saddle bridges in acoustic guitars. It works the same way as round piezo discs that many cigar box guitar builders use,

but is much better at delivering balanced acoustic tones in a live concert setting.

This setup also includes a battery-powered preamp and EQ, which is essential to the whole setup. Without a preamp, any piezo pickup is just an underpowered contact mic that sounds like a fart box. Always use a preamp with a piezo pickup. *Always!*

Prepare your cigar box guitar neck exactly as shown in the previous chapter, with one exception: When notching the neck, make the raised notch in the middle (where the

PHOTO: DAVID SUTTON

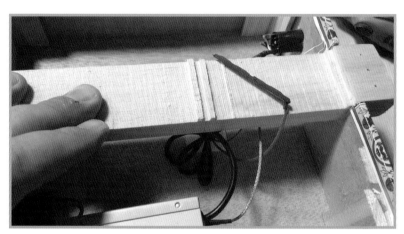

Figure 3-1.

Figure 3-2.

Figure 3-3.

bridge rests) at least ⅜" (1 cm) wide. Cut a groove in the middle of that notch just wide and deep enough to fit the piezo rod pickup (Figure 3-1).

The piezo rod should be flush with the raised notch or raised up ¹⁄₁₆" (1½ mm) at the most (Figure 3-2). The top of the pickup should never fall below the notched wood. It will need to make contact with the underside of the cigar box lid in order to transfer sound vibrations to the preamp.

Plug the piezo rod jack into the installed pickup unit (Figure 3-3). Test the setup before closing the box lid by loading a 9V battery into the preamp and plugging it into a guitar amp. Turn everything on and tap the pickup. If you can hear it through the guitar amp, everything is set and ready to go.

Install the cigar box lid and finish the rest of the guitar as shown in the previous chapter.

*Note: Originally, this pickup system was intended to be mounted on the upper bout of an acoustic guitar, as evidenced by the curved side of the preamp's face. When properly installed, the face of the preamp will still retain the curve. It's just a small aesthetic price to pay for improving your amplified tone.*

## Personalizing the Neck: Adding Text

Every great cowboy singer had his name inlaid up the neck of his guitar, from Jimmie Rogers to Merle Haggard. I think cowboy singers are cool, so I created my own way of personalizing the necks of my cigar box guitars with a woodburning pen.

My dad gave me a pyrography kit when I was 10 that included some thin pieces of wood, carbon paper, sample designs to trace, and a low-powered woodburning pen. It would take at least ten minutes before the pen was nice and hot, and even then it was slow going to get nice, dark lines.

When I started making cigar box guitars in the mid 1990s, I remembered that woodburning kit and used the pen to draw fret lines onto my instruments. It took forever, but it looked great. Now that I build many guitars, I've invested in a professional woodburning station that ran about $120. It was a big investment, especially for building these poor man's guitars, but it paid off in the time I saved and the overall looks when finished. Professional setups heat up within seconds, produce a red hot tip, and allow you to personalize a neck in one-tenth of the time.

Besides, the older I get, the more I become a tool hoarder. New tools are fun and make it a delight to go into the woodshop to build. When in doubt, buy the better tool.

My personalized necks have the text running up the face. The actual fret line markers are positioned on the side so that only the player can see them.

I build the guitar exactly the same as shown in the previous chapter, except I draw the fret lines on the side. This means I retain the same 23" (58½ cm) scale length and then just woodburn the frets (see Figure 3-4) as ⅛" (⅓ cm) guide lines with small dot markers at the 3/5/7/9/12 frets, etc.

**TOOLS:**
- Woodburning pen
- Carbon paper
- Home printer and standard paper
- Pencil

Figure 3-4.

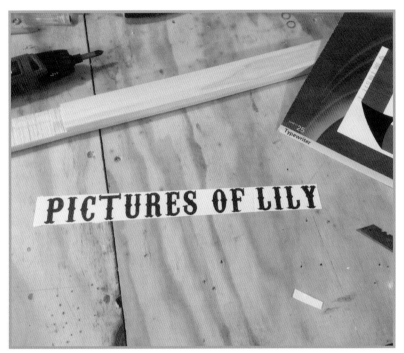

Figure 3-5.

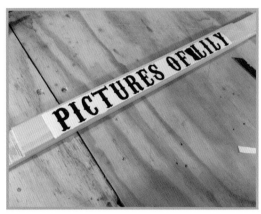

Figure 3-6.

Figure 3-7.

Figure 3-8.

### LAYING OUT THE TEXT

*Note: You will need to have the cigar box guitar neck fully notched out and sanded before adding the text.*

Measure the face of neck to see how much space is available for text. In this Pictures of Lily guitar, I had a space that was 16" (40½ cm) wide and 1¾" (4½ cm) high. Your text should leave a little blank space on the neck for the best look. I usually allow at least 1½" (3¾ cm) of blank space on each side of the text and at least ¼" (⅔ cm) above and below (Figure 3-5).

Now that you know how much real estate is available on the face of the neck, use your home computer and printer to experiment with different fonts and sizes. You may need to use two pieces of standard paper to fill the length of the text, as seen here. Just line them up and tape them together (Figure 3-6).

Figure 3-9.

Center the text on the face of the neck, slip a piece of carbon paper underneath, and trace over the text outline. Use masking tape to hold everything in place as you work (Figure 3-7).

When you remove the paper and carbon paper, you should have clear lines as guides for woodburning (Figure 3-8).

Fire up the woodburning pen and fill in the text (Figure 3-9). Take your time. It looks best to keep all fill lines going in the same direction. Following the wood grain gives you the best results.

Once you're finished, apply polyurethane and complete the guitar. And then go buy a cowboy hat and tooled leather chaps.

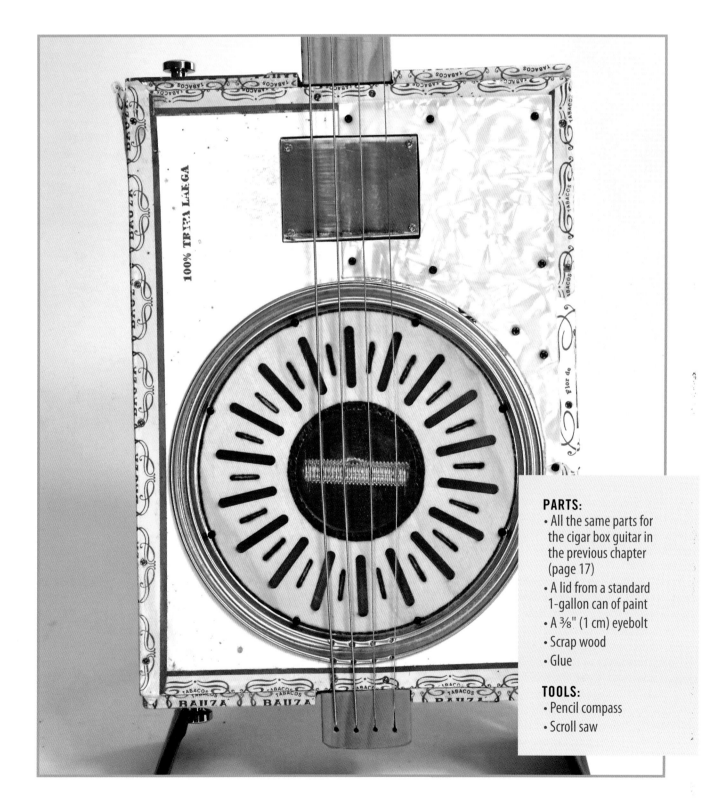

**PARTS:**
- All the same parts for the cigar box guitar in the previous chapter (page 17)
- A lid from a standard 1-gallon can of paint
- A ⅜" (1 cm) eyebolt
- Scrap wood
- Glue

**TOOLS:**
- Pencil compass
- Scroll saw

### Poor Man's Dobro: Paint Can Lid Resonator Cone

Using a common paint can lid as a dobro cone was the invention of Matty Baratto back in the 1990s. Baratto has been building Cigfiddles, his own unique brand of cigar box guitars, for almost 25 years in his North Hollywood workshop, Baratto Guitars. They're played by Paul McCartney, Johnny Depp, Steven Tyler, and countless other A-list celebrities.

Matty is also one of the nicest guys I've ever met.

With the exception of inserting commercial-spun aluminum resonator cones to a cigar box guitar, adding regular metal to the soundboard (box lid) simply adds a trashiness to the tone. Mind you, trashiness is awesome and more trashiness is divine. However, if you're looking for that authentic Dobro guitar tone, this ain't the right dance for ya. Painted lid guitars are for us trash addicts!

In the previous chapter, the bridge was positioned 4¼" (10¾ cm) from the end of the poplar stick. If positioned correctly, the paint lid can sit in the box and still have the bridge rest exactly in the center of the lid.

Choose a cigar box that is wide enough to accept the paint lid. There should be at least a ½" (1¼ cm) space left on each side of the lid. Take the lid off the paint can. Using the paint can opening, measure the inside diameter of the opening. This is the diameter you'll want to cut out of the box top. This will make sure the lid fits perfectly into the box, snapping into place. Without the lid, measure the opening.

Position the lid so that it is on the left side of the box with the inside lip of the lid ½" (1¼ cm) from the left side of the cigar box lid (Figure 3-10).

Mark the box at the center of the lid position. Set the pencil compass to half the diameter of the measurement above to give

Figure 3-10.

Figure 3-11.

you the radius. Draw the circle on the lid (Figure 3-11). Carefully remove the box lid from the box and cut out the hole using a scroll saw.

Figure 3-12.

Figure 3-13.

Figure 3-14.

Place the lid in the hole you just cut (Figure 3-12). It should fit snugly and pop into place.

Notching out the neck to fit the lid: You will not need a raised notch at the bridge location when using a paint lid. However, you may need to dig a little deeper into the neck to accept the lip of the paint lid, as shown here (Figure 3-13).

The downside to routing deep pockets in the neck is that the string tension can warp the neck. In order to ensure a solid neck, glue a scrap piece of wood to the underside of the neck (Figure 3-14). Make sure the scrap wood is cut to fit inside the cigar box.

Now that the lid fits the box and the neck fits into the lid, continue building the rest of the guitar according to the previous chapter (pages 15–45).

I added a decorative wood resonator cone cover to my paint lid for this guitar (Figure 3-15). The cover is from *www.CBGitty.com* and was meant for an actual handspun resonator cone. I merely trimmed the edges of the wood to fit on the inside of the paint lid and used small guitar tuner screws to hold it in place. It adds nothing to the tone and playability of the instrument, but it looks hella cool.

Because the paint lid sits a little lower into the lid, you will need a thicker threaded bolt as a bridge (Figure 3-16). I cut a ⅜" (1 cm) eye bolt to a 1¾" (4½ cm) length and used it as a bridge. (I had a pile of these eyebolts to make the washtub bass in chapter 6.)

**Note:** Notice that this photo shows the guitar with fret markers and a finished neck. That's because I messed this guitar up with the deep routes and only discovered it after I strung it up and played it at a gig. As I performed, the guitar slowly bowed, knocking the tuning out for the entire set. Ugh . . . I went home, took it apart, and fixed it.

Cigar box guitar building is always trial and error. If it doesn't play right at first, rebuild it into something better.

Figure 3-15.

Figure 3-16.

## OTHER NOTES ON THIS GUITAR

The pickup: My shop is filled with parts gathered over years of collecting. The pickup was handmade by the late Dan Sleep of Humidor Guitars. He had recently passed away, and I had the honor of performing at his memorial. He was known for these flat humbucking pickups, and I used to buy 'em by the dozen. I have a few remaining in my shop and save them for the most special guitars.

This pickup was designed to be flat, allowing for a shallow route into a cigar box guitar. You can add standard guitar pickups in the same way, but they will require deep routes like the paint lid. You will need to build up the internal bracing of the neck just like I did above. Experiment. Try anything and everything.

The pickguard: The gorgeous pearloid pickguard (see Figure 3-17) is actually drum wrap taken from a vintage drum set. You can also buy this stuff new. It's easy to cut and looks fantastic.

Figure 3-17.

Figure 3-18.

The addition of a fourth string: Although the previous chapter shows a cigar box guitar with three strings, a standard stick of poplar can actually handle the tension of four guitar strings.

For this guitar, I added a high B string, allowing the guitar to be string in Open G Major (GDGB, low to high). To add an extra string, you just add one more tuner and drill four string anchor holes instead of three. The strings are spaced ⅜" (1 cm) apart from each other.

I also used this setup for the Pictures of Lily guitar, which has an internal piezo rod pickup and preamp, as shown above (Figure 3-18). Because the nut and bridge are threaded bolts, the design allows for three- or four-string spacing options.

I had the paint lid perfectly embedded in the cigar box and the hand-wound pickup wired up. The polyurethane on the neck was tacky enough to start stringing it up. (There are only a few fingerprints embedded in it.)

### Builder's Diary: "The Hobo Guitar"

I often approach cigar box guitar building as a fiction writer might approach writing a story, weaving mythical tales into the design of the guitar. To accomplish certain looks, I keep a huge stash of old yardsticks, tin cans, and other found objects in my shop that I frequently cull from.

As I build, I start imagining the backstory to the art guitar. Where was the builder from? What kind of music did he play? Why did he use this old tin can as a sound hole?

The sound hole is a rusty can lid with the original can opener holes serving as sound holes. The fretboard is an antique advertising yardstick featuring a phone number so old, it reads, "10-R-4." Topping it all off is an old Gilbert's Cigars box from the 1920s. (The cigar box guitar has a tone that sounds like an old 78 record!)

This cigar box guitar is hours old, yet it appears to be straight out of a Depression-Era shantytown.

The sides of the neck are covered in hobo symbols.

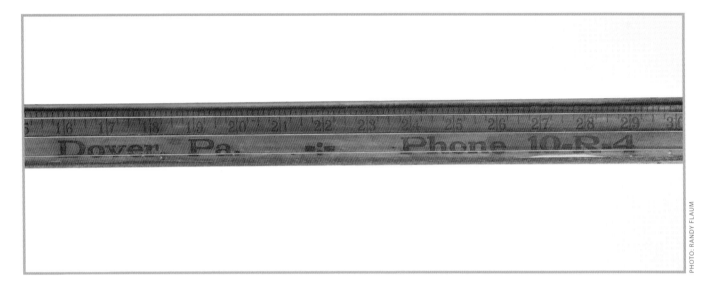

PHOTO: RANDY FLAUM

For this particular instrument, my fictitious legend unfolds like this:

Scrap Johnny was often seen pushing a cart on the dusty back roads of a small Pennsylvania town. He'd collect tin cans, metal scraps, and anything else he could turn in for pennies to survive. Times were tough in the 1930s. His clothes were tattered and the lines on his face were a lot deeper than they should have been for a 17-year-old.

But strange as it was, that kid was always singing.

Johnny cobbled a guitar together from things in his cart. A tin can, an empty cigar box, and yardstick came together to make a crude three-string guitar. He burned hobo symbols into it using a hot nail heated over a candle. He learned the code symbols from the train travelers.

That cigar box guitar was probably his only true possession.

He loved the train that came through town and would use the chugging sound as his metronome when he sang. "Hallelujah, I'm a Bum!" and other travel songs were in his short repertoire. Johnny would talk to the 'bos who were on their way to New York City or other faraway destinations, asking about the big towns, prying them for good stories.

It must have been around the summer of 1937 when locals stopped seeing Scrap Johnny scavenging around the neighborhood. Somebody found his rusty old cart abandoned by the railroad tracks, but nobody was completely sure where he went. Eventually, most people forgot about the young scrapper and his cobbled guitar.

Half a century later, a Chicago moving company is relocating the contents of a mansion from a recently deceased musician. The man was a star of radio that, years ago, seemed to appear from nowhere. The workers wrap and pack the dust covered belongings: gold records, tailored stage clothes, photos of the biggest celebrities of the 1940s and 1950s, a laminated musician's union card, and several instruments. Reaching under the bed, one worker pulls out a crude guitar, cobbled from a cigar box, covered in hobo symbols, and sporting a tin can for the sound hole.

***Not all legends are written in books. Sometimes they're written inside the instruments we make.***

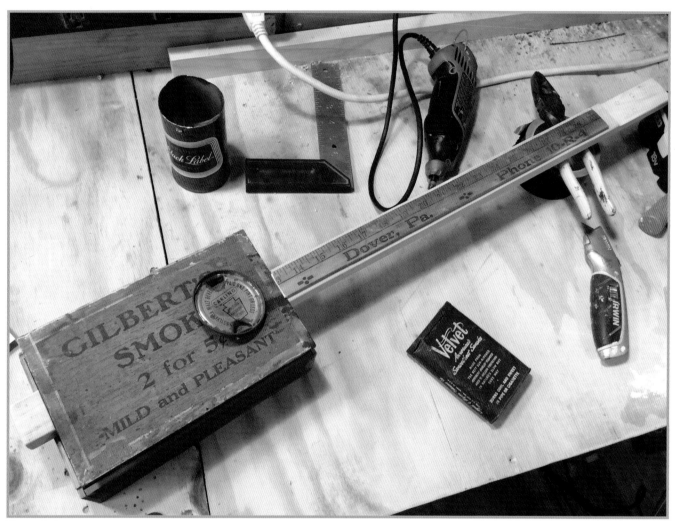

Figure 3-19.

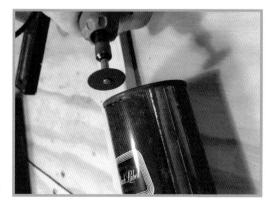

Figure 3-20.

**BUILDING NOTES**

The guitar was built with the same neck-through design as above (Figure 3-19).

To get the sound hole, I removed the lid of an old rusted beer can using a rotary tool cutoff wheel (Figure 3-20). I positioned it on the box so that the two original holes would fall outside of where the stick goes through the box. I traced the triangle holes with a pencil and cut them out of the box using a rotary tool with a cutting bit. I hot glued

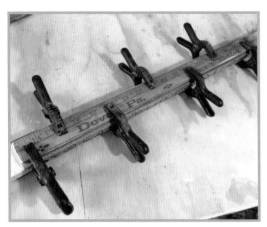

Figure 3-21.

Figure 3-22.

Figure 3-23.

Figure 3-24.

the can lid to the top and secured it with a couple tiny guitar tuner screws.

The fretboard is an antique yardstick. It's simply glued it to the neck, using a bunch of clamps to hold it in place (Figure 3-21). This guitar has no fret markers and is played by feel. (Unfretted necks are a great way to develop your ears as a slide player.)

Because the fretboard and tin can are raised, I needed to heighten the bridge so the strings would clear. I simply used a scrap piece of the yardstick to fit under the bolt bridge (Figure 3-22).

Here's an alternate version of a string tree. I took small eyehooks and screwed them into the headstock. I then placed a bolt into the eyes. It pulls the strings down past the nut, keeping them in place (Figure 3-23).

A quick Internet search gave me a wealth of information on hobo symbols. I chose my favorites and woodburned them all over the neck for an added touch (Figure 3-24).

## Builder's Diary: Damned If I Do – Electric Resonator Cigar Box Guitar

Last week, I stepped into my woodshop with the goal of capturing struggle, poverty, and the Blues within the artistic side of cigar box guitar building. I put a CD of Crying Sam Collins & His Gitfiddle in the stereo and started scanning my parts bins for mean and deadly-looking parts.

This guitar would be built with a large wooden Punch Cigars box. The bigger the box, the better the sound—and I wanted this one to be a good sounding guitar. The neck would be poplar, a poor-man's alternative to maple, but always a great choice for a slide guitar since warping isn't a factor.

I needed parts, and my woodshop is filled from top to bottom with random parts. The first thing to jump out at me were these skull sound hole covers. OK, so this guitar would

have death as a theme. But those Crying Sam Collins songs were demanding something more: something creaky, out-of-tune (as often was his guitar), and poverty-stricken. This instrument needed to be 100% lo-fi and trashy.

On the shelf in my woodshop, I have a stack of 5" (12¾ cm) mini baking pans from the 1950s. These little metal pieces make wonderful cigar box dobro cones and have a smaller footprint than paint can lids. I had found my first set in a thrift store and now I scour eBay for them every day. After cutting the huge hole in the box, I installed it with some tiny guitar tuner peg screws.

With a rusted baking pan as a resonator and skulls for sound holes, I needed the right pickup to make it electric. I chose the cheap acoustic sound hole pickup from *www.GoldFoil.com*. Its low profile fits right on the pan without any extra routing.

Figure 3-25.

Figure 3-26.

## Extra: How to Mod a *GoldFoil.com* Acoustic Pickup to Become a Top-Mounted Electric Pickup:

Remove the cover and then paint it. (Optional—not shown) I used Rust-Oleum® dark brown textured paint for a rust look.

Remove the bottom mounting tabs by grinding them off on a belt sander. Once you grind through the rivets, pry the tabs off. Grind the rest of the rivet base off of the pickup (Figure 3-25, above).

Bend the side tabs down with a pair of pliers (Figure 3-26). Be careful, the tabs are made of cheap metal and can easily break in the wrong place.

Cut the tabs off with a hacksaw, leaving enough metal on each side of the pickup to become mounting tabs (Figure 3-27). Use a file or belt sander to gently remove sharp corners on the tabs.

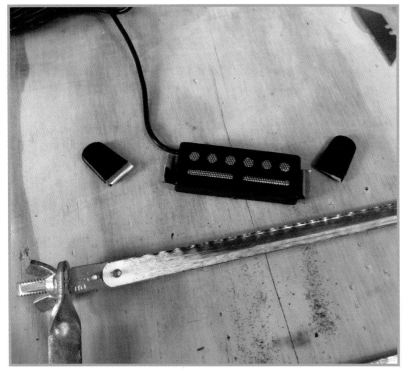

Figure 3-27.

## Big Joe Williams' Homemade Instruments

**EXCERPTED FROM *AFRICAN AMERICAN FOLK ART AND CRAFTS*, EDITED BY WILLIAM FERRIS**

Blues singer Big Joe Williams recalls from his childhood playing a single strand of cotton-baling wire strung on a wall between two staples with spools for bridges. Variation in pitch was obtained by sliding an empty bottle along the string. Other instruments he recalls from his childhood were a two-stringed cigar box guitar, a cane fife, a set of pan pipes or "quills," and an upturned bucket, which served as a drum. As an adult he switched to a six-string and finally a nine-string guitar.

Figure 3-28.

Figure 3-29.

Figure 3-30.

Drill ¹⁄₁₆" (1½ mm) screw holes in the new mounting tabs (Figure 3-28).

Cut the pre-wired cord to the length needed. Strip the outer insulation, exposing the inside wires (Figure 3-29).

Solder the wires to a ¼" (⅔ cm) guitar jack, white to the lead and ground wires to the ground lug connected to the inside sleeve of the guitar jack (Figure 3-30).

The neck was the last piece of the puzzle in this desperation blues guitar. I wanted to woodburn a phrase, saying, or several words that captured the essence of the blues (Figure 3-31). The challenge was to avoid blues clichés about voodoo or mojo.

And then I heard something coming from the stereo . . .

*'Cus I ain't got no lovin' baby now.*
*I'd rather see my coffin come rollin' in*
*my door.*

*Hear my woman say, that she don't want me no more, Lord.*
*I ain't got no lovin' baby now.*

Crying Sam was singing "Graveyard Digger's Blues"—sorrowful and resigned. Between the Jim Crow laws at the time, utter poverty, and, like this song, suffering the loss of a woman, these bluesmen were living the phrase, "damned if I do, damned if I don't." Ol' Crying Sam would rather see his own coffin than to hear a woman tell him she didn't want him anymore. *Whoa . . .*

And that was it. I pulled out the woodburning pen and burned "Damned if I do..." in an old typewriter font up the neck.

One last touch was to use a door handle as a bridge cover.

It's the essence of desperation blues.

The neck got several coats of polyurethane, tuners were added, and the instrument was assembled. When I plugged it into the small practice amp in my shop, I got goose bumps. The tone was a gumbo of metallic creaking, electric snarl, and graveyard moan.

Always listen to music when building instruments. Search out the deep music in order to make deep guitars.

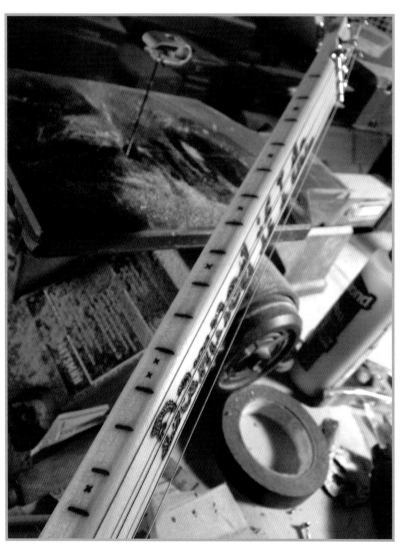

Figure 3-31.

## Robert Johnson's Three-String Diddley Bow

### EXCERPTED FROM *GUITAR PLAYER* MAGAZINE, SEPT. 1990

Wink Clark described Robert playing a three-string diddley bow that he fashioned by driving nails into a wall, attaching strands of wire to the nails, and using bottles as bridges and a slider: "He'd put him a bottle under the wires at the bottom and top, push 'em up tight, and it was just like tunin' a guitar. He could play what he was singin', but I never could get no sense out of it."

# CHAPTER 4:
## "The Portland Cowboy" Tin Can Guitar

At the top of every cigar box guitar I use in concert, I tape a list of songs for each individual guitar. Since my band never has a set list, these little notes of paper serve as a guide for me. I'll pick up a guitar, scan the songs, choose one that is perfect for the energy in the room, and then launch into it.

### PARTS:
- Olive oil tin can or similar size can
- 12 steel wire staples, sized 1" x ⅞" (2½ x 2¼ cm). (I bought a big bag of these on eBay.) These staples will take the place of the twisted wire frets. I didn't have 30-gauge copper wire, so I used the staple fret idea from the Horse's Bridle guitar (pages 12–13) as my inspiration.
- Two guitar tuners, one right and one left
- Two guitar strings, acoustic G and B strings
- ¾" x 1" x 26" (2 x 2½ x 66 cm) piece of scrap wood (I used maple)
- Two machine screws, size ¼" (⅔ cm)-20 x 1" (2½ cm)
- Two small round-head wood screws

### TOOLS:
- Drill and drill bits: ⁵⁄₁₆" (¾ cm) and ¹⁄₁₆" (1½ mm)
- Pencil
- Hammer
- Rotary tool and routing bit or file

My quest to discover a guitar music one-step deeper than the Delta Blues led me to the cigar box guitar. But what about the rest of the band?

Just about every band I have put together since the early 2000s has consisted of mostly homemade instruments in order to deliver hellfire trash blues. The goal isn't to play old time music; it's to create new sounds using old technology. One critic said of my band, "If Rob Zombie had a jug band, it would sound like this."

I lead my current band by playing cigar box guitar, singing, and kicking a Foot Stomper as a bass drum. Shane Speal & the Snakes includes band members "Farmer" Jon Sprenkle on electric washtub bass, Derick Kemper on harmonica and beer can mic, Rick Stepina on hand percussion, and sometimes Ronn Benway on washboard. Each of the instruments in this section have been used by the band and were tested on recordings, in barrooms, and festival stages. They're set up for minimal feedback and maximum tone.

These are all our secrets.

I found that my little song list was nothing original when I acquired this two-string tin can guitar from the 1930s. I bought it from eBay; it had been recently discovered in Portland, Oregon without any backstory. Among the wear marks, sweat stains, and rust on this heavily used instrument is a 1½" x 2" (3¾ x 5 cm) piece of paper glued to the side. It was the musician's original set list!

• Theme – Back on the Texas Plains
• Medley – When it's Springtime
• Smile the While
• You Tell Me Your Dream
• Bob – Boy Chew; Chink Drive
• Cuddle Up a Little Closer
• Medley – Wash. Lee; Gold Coast; Wash. Lee
• Vocal – Baby Needs
• Theme Back on the Texas Plains

Figure 4-1.

With a little research and some help from fellow folk music historian, Ben "Gitty" Baker, I was able to piece together the set list details.

- "Texas Plains" – A cowboy song originally performed by Stuart Hamblin in 1935
- "When It's Springtime in the Rockies" – made famous by Gene Autry in 1937
- "Smile the While" – also known as "Till We Meet Again," originally published in 1918
- "You Tell Me Your Dream, I'll Tell You Mine" – words by Seymour Rice and Albert H. Brown, music by Charles N. Daniels 1899
- "Cuddle Up A Little Closer, Lovey Mine" – Music written by Karl Hoschna, lyrics by Otto Harbach. Published in 1908. Ada Jones and Billy Murray

- "Washington and Lee Swing" is a school fight song written in 1910 that has been used by General Grant High School in Portland OR as well as many other schools
- "Gold Coast Express" is a cowboy yodeling song by Patsy Montana and Prairie Ramblers, recorded in 1935

The only part of the set list I couldn't track down was Bob – Boy Chew; Chink Drive. Something tells me that Bob was a character in the show and these two selections were possibly scenes in the show, or they are original songs and not covers.

As I hold this guitar, I think about the cowboy and yodeling songs. I envision a singer in a cowboy hat stepping up to a radio microphone to perform his songs while strumming this guitar, or perhaps a student

Figure 4-2.

Figure 4-3.

in a school show, playing a down-and-out character.

The guitar is fantastically simple in design, showing pure genius in the builder. It's just a simple stick mounted on top of a Tea Garden Syrup tin using two screws. The twelve frets are copper wire, approximately 30 gauge, and are hand-twisted at the proper fret marks for an 18" (45¾ cm) scale instrument; a small piece of coat hanger serves as the nut. The floating bridge is long gone. I placed a small bolt where the original bridge was seated just to see if the instrument actually played. Indeed, it did, loudly and mostly in tune!

The original story may have been lost to the hands of time, but that doesn't stop me from recreating the guitar for my own future songs! I decided to make my own so that I can explore all the songs on that original set list. Here's how I built my own version.

The original tin guitar had an 18" (45¾ cm) scale with almost 7" (17¾ cm) of extra room behind the bridge (Figure 4-1). I kept with the same measurements just to be sure. I chose a scrap piece of maple I had in my shop as the neck.

Drill two holes for guitar tuners at one end of the neck using a ⁵⁄₁₆" (¾ cm) drill bit (Figure 4-2). At the opposite end of the neck, mark two string anchor holes ½" (1¼ cm) from the end of the stick. Use a ¹⁄₁₆" (1½ mm) bit and drill straight.

Mark a line 2½" (6⅓ cm) from the end of the headstock (Figure 4-3). This will be the location of the nut. Measure 18" (45¾ cm) from the nut line and mark a second line for the bridge.

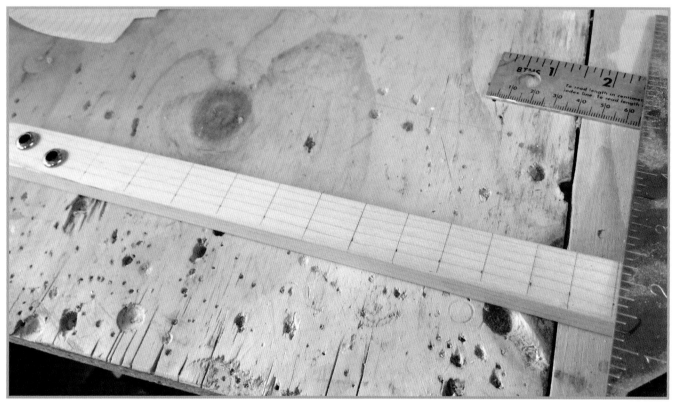

Figure 4-4.

Figure 4-5.

Mark twelve fret lines (Figure 4-4). Use these simplified measurements, starting at the nut:

- 1" (2½ cm)
- 2" (5 cm)
- 2⅞" (7⅓ cm)
- 3¾" (9½ cm)
- 4½" (11½ cm)
- 5¼" (13⅓ cm)
- 6" (15¼ cm)
- 6⅝" (16¾ cm)
- 7¼" (18⅓ cm)
- 7⅞" (20 cm)
- 8½" (21½ cm)
- 9" (22¾ cm)

Place one staple at each fret line, skipping the line for the nut (Figure 4-5).

Figure 4-6.

Turn the neck over and gently hammer the ends of the staples, bending them over into the back of the neck. A small dead blow fretting hammer works great (pictured, Figure 4-6), but any hammer will do. Turn the neck back over and double check the positioning of the staple frets. You should be able to tap them forward or backward if they've slipped away from the lines.

At the headstock, gently tap in the bushings for the guitar tuners. Turn the neck over and install the tuners (Figure 4-7). Remember, as you are positioning them make sure the brass gears are pointed *toward* the body of the guitar.

Figure 4-7.

Figure 4-8.

Figure 4-9.

Cut a nut slot in the neck for the bolt (Figure 4-8). I used a rotary tool and routing bit. You can use a file, as well.

Position the neck over the tin can, leaving about 4" (10 cm) of the neck sticking out of the back end (Figure 4-9).

Turn the whole thing over and mark lines at the beginning and end of the can lip (Figure 4-10).

Using a ¹⁄₁₆" (1½ mm) drill bit, drill pilot holes in the center of each line (Figure 4-11).

Place the tin can back on the neck and screw in one round head screw at each end of the tin can lip (Figure 4-12). The head of the screw is what secures the neck to the

Figure 4-10.

Figure 4-11.

Figure 4-12.

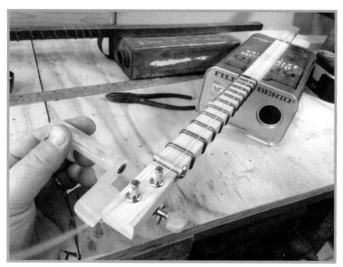

Figure 4-13.

can, just like the antique guitar. Tighten the screws to make sure the can doesn't move. If the screws are too far away from the lip, add washers.

String it up with the B and E strings. Place the bolts in the bridge and nut positions (Figure 4-13).

Tuning: The antique guitar still has its original strings on it. I was able to tighten them to an open A power chord (A, E low to high). The tuning works well for the new version, as well.

One of these days, I'm gonna learn all those songs on that old set list!

See videos of both guitars in action at *www.PoorMansGuitar.com/TinCan.*

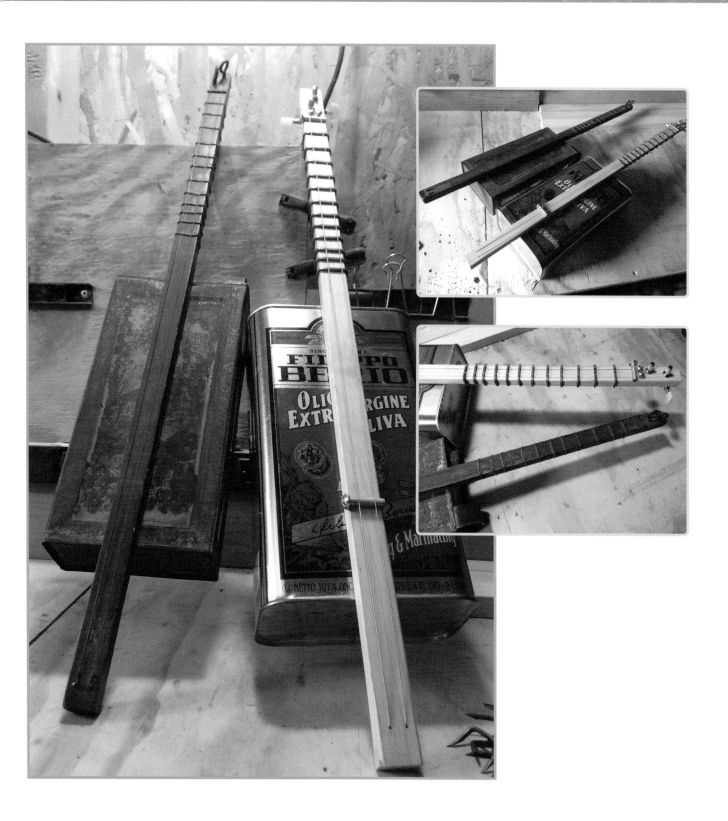

## Guitarcheology: One-String Violin, Circa 1940

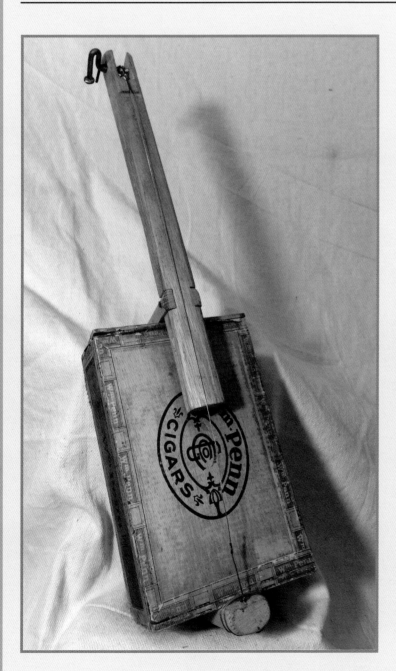

This one-string violin was discovered somewhere in Minnesota. As with so many of these antique instruments, the history is long gone. It features an oak neck that runs *around* the box without any connection or bracing to the box itself.

Simple box joints connect the neck to the body mounts.

The box is a Wm. Penn 5-cent cigar box from the 1930s or 1940s and contains no sound holes or any other tooling.

One very cool detail is the bent nail tuner. The unknown builder took a 16-penny (89

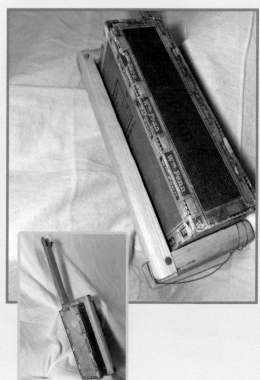

mm) nail and bent it into a worm-shaped tuner. A small Allen wrench is also jammed into the tuner hole to keep the nail from moving. The guitar is strung with a single violin string.

A closer look reveals that the builder used power tools to create this, with cleanly cut box joints and a flattened fretboard. Unlike other antiques in my collection, this one has very little sweat and wear marks on it, suggesting that the fiddle might not have worked as well as they had intended. In fact, comparing the wear on the box to the construction of the neck, I suspect that the builder used a box that had been lying around for quite some time. The face of the cigar box is sun bleached, but the bleach marks do not darken under the neck.

This artwork (below right) from a 1940s calendar shows a boy playing a similar one-string violin. Notice the tuning peg, which is constantly held on the left hand and changes the string pitch as he plays.

Unidentified fiddler playing his homemade instrument. Savannah, GA, circa 1898.

# Newspaper Article: George S. Conway's Oyster Can Violin and Cigar Box Violin

Music can hit you like a sledgehammer, causing your entire being to point toward a mystical instrument and possessing you to build one. It's happened to me over and over again, and it happened to George S. Conway almost 150 years ago. As a young boy, he heard a violin and had to have one. At the time, he only had an oyster can to use as the fiddle body, so he used it.

According to the *Newark (OH) Daily Advocate*, November 26, 1914 article:

*One night, a dance was given at the home where [Conway] was employed and to the amazement of the child, a queer looking wooden box with strings on it furnished the music for the dancers. This was his first acquaintance with the violin and so closely did he cling to the side of the fiddler and . . . so many questions did he ask that the musician was hampered in his efforts to play for the dance and the little boy was hurriedly sent to bed. But he still dreamed of the "music box" and the next morning found an old oyster can and made himself a fiddle.*

*Later, he secured a cigar box and some strings, and this second effort was a great improvement over the first one. So busily did he fiddle on the new instrument that the members of the family became greatly annoyed and his endeavors had to cease.*

Conway would eventually start his own violin shop in Newark, Ohio, producing over 250 instruments in his lifetime. At the time of the 1914 newspaper article, Conway was commanding $150 to $500 for his Stradivarius and Guarneri styled violins. Those prices translate to $3,700 to $12,300 in today's money!

# CHAPTER 5: "Foot Stomper"
# Cigar Box Percussion Unit

### The Birth of the Foot Stomper

This all started with the worst gig of my life
. . . and the birth of my quest for a perfect
foot drum instrument.

In 2009, I had been invited to headline
a concert at the Southside Film Festival
in Bethlehem, Pennsylvania, to coincide
with the screening of *Songs Inside the Box*, a
cigar box guitar documentary by acclaimed
filmmaker Max Shores. I was the central
figure in the film and was booked to appear
with several other musicians who also
appeared in the documentary.

I had prepared a one-man band show
where I was seated with my cigar box
guitar and an old bass drum at my feet,
pounding out the rhythm like Hasil Adkins.
Unfortunately, what emanated from the
stage was a pathetic slop of amateur music,
not worthy for an open mic stage, let alone a
headliner gig. The audience started checking
out by my second song and the harder I tried
to play, the more invisible I was to them. By
the end of the show, I was just an asshole
kicking a drum and slashing at a cigar box
guitar. It was cringe-worthy.

After packing my gear, I was faced with
a long three-hour drive home. I could have
beat myself up the entire time, but I shoved
my crushed spirit into the backseat and
proceeded to logically critique my show. I
knew it was necessary to strip down my
entire playing style and rebuild it. But how?

When I got home, I started dialing in
every YouTube video of one-man bands
that I respected. I noticed that artists like
Ben Prestage, Richard Johnston, and Seasick

Years of late-night practice is what makes author Shane Speal the undisputed "King of the Cigar Box Guitar."

PHOTO: JOHN MCELLIGOTT

A horrible, horrible setup. Here I am, performing with a preacher's bass drum, held up by cement blocks.

PHOTO: AMY MUMMERT

PHOTO: JOHN MCELLIGOTT

Foot Stomper prototype #1, built from a 7Up crate, old floorboards found in my garage, and a few piezo discs hidden inside. It was routed into an external preamp and then the PA system. Not perfect, but a good start toward a better sound.

Steve had their entire bodies in sync as they performed. Their cigar box guitars and foot drums were like machine cogs moving in one continuous motion. And they all had rollicking *swing* to them; the guitar was as much a percussion instrument that would blend in with whatever foot percussion they were using.

The *swing* was the key!

For myself, I realized that the big bass drum I was using was just too physical in nature. Violently banging my leg up and down on the drum pedal was just too much action to keep my own swing in check. I needed something that would amplify a foot tap, turning it into a booming stomp. I needed something more physically subtle, so I took a tip from Seasick Steve's homemade "Mississippi Drum Machine" stomper (his is just an empty box with a drum mic inside) and made my own version. The first prototype was assembled from a Coca Cola crate, a few floorboards, and internal contact mic piezo discs.

In the last decade, I have continued to refine the setup into these plans that are shown here. When dialed up correctly in a PA system, this foot stomper will sound like a combat boot to the chest. I've used this instrument in festivals where it was cranked so loud it sounded like cannons going off.

And all you need to do is tap on it with your foot.

The concept of the Foot Stomper is so simple, I feel like a criminal for withholding the secrets of its construction all these years! It's nothing more than a few electrified contact pickups (the piezo discs) with boosted bass from the preamp and plugged into a PA system with 100% bass, no midrange and no treble. Many people have tried to build their own stompers, but they always forget the preamp.

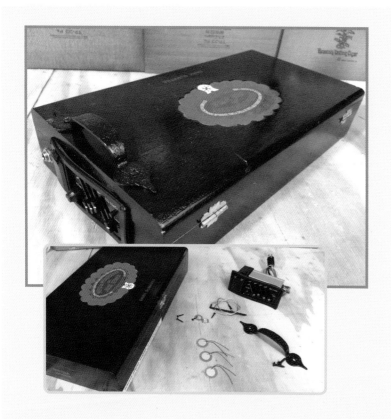

**PARTS:**
- Long cigar box with a depth of at least 2¼" (5¾ cm) (Choose boxes with thick lids so they can sustain the punishment of stomping)
- Acoustic guitar preamp and piezo rod pickup (See Chapter 3 on page 46)*
- Three 20 mm piezo disks with pre-wired leads
- Door handle (optional)

**TOOLS:**
- Coping saw or rotary tool
- Soldering iron and solder and shrink tubing
- Drill and ⅜" (1 cm) bit
- Hot glue gun and glue sticks

*Note: You may notice certain electronics or parts repeated throughout this book, such as this preamp. If certain parts work in one type of instrument, I try them in others. I always have a drawer full of these preamps in my shop because they enhance signal strength well and they're cheap.

A Foot Stomper without a preamp will sound like tap-tap-tapping. Add a preamp and boost the bass and you'll shake the walls and rattle the windows.

*Remember, a piezo pickup without a preamp is nothing but a fart box.*

The electronics for the Foot Stomper require you to hack the pickup by cutting off the piezo rod and attaching three piezo discs to the cord. Start by cutting off the piezo rod pickup directly under the black sheathing (Figure 5-1). Throw the rod pickup away and save the wire. Separate the hot (white wire) and ground (braided wire) and strip ¼" (⅔ cm) of insulation off the white wire.

Solder all three black wires from the piezo disks to the braided ground wire (Figure 5-2). Slip a 1" (2½ cm) piece of shrink tubing onto the wire and then solder all three red wires from the piezo disks to the white wire. Slide the tubing over the solder joint and heat to shrink.

Cut a 3½" x 1½" (9 x 3¾ cm) hole in the box to fit the preamp (Figure 5-3). You can use a coping saw, carpenter's knife, or a Dremel rotary tool with a cutting disk. Make sure the preamp fits inside, but do not mount it yet.

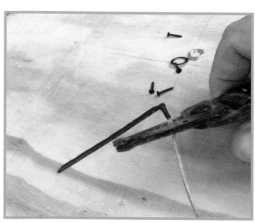

Figure 5-1.

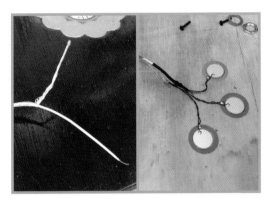

Figure 5-2.

Figure 5-3.

Figure 5-4.

Figure 5-5.

Drill a ⅜" (1 cm) hole beside the preamp for the guitar jack (Figure 5-4). Depending on the thickness of the box sides, you may need to use a rotary tool to thin the wood from the backside in order to allow the guitar jack to go the whole way through.

The piezo disk pickups will be placed on the underside of the box lid, on the opposite side of the preamp (Figure 5-5). Scuff up the underside of the box lid with a scrap of sandpaper to help the hot glue adhere properly.

Position the discs in a triangle and hot glue them to the underside of the box lid (Figure 5-6). Make sure to glue the metal side of the disc to the lid, not the ceramic side. Don't be stingy with the glue; put a lot on there to hold the discs and wires in place.

Figure 5-6.

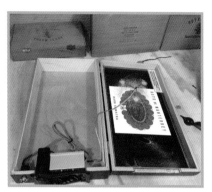

Figure 5-7.

Figure 5-8.

Figure 5-9.

Plug the piezo wire into the preamp and install the guitar jack (Figure 5-7). Carefully hot glue all sides of the cigar box and close the lid shut.

Mount the preamp to the box with the screws provided (Figure 5-8).

(Optional) Mount an old door handle to the edge of the box, as shown (Figure 5-9).

This will provide an easy way to pull the stomper back to position with your heel if it starts to move around stage. You may also want to add non-slip material to the bottom, such as rubber feet or cut a section of rubber door mat and hot glue it to the underside.

## Playing Your Foot Stomper

This Foot Stomper works best when plugged into a PA system. Guitar and bass amps just don't provide the "combat boot to the chest" tone that a PA with 15" (38 cm) speakers can deliver. Dial the preamp to 100% bass with no midrange, no treble, and no presence. Plug the stomper into the PA and dial in the tones the same way on the mixing board. When this instrument is cranked, it'll only need slight taps to get it thumping like a Godzilla movie.

### VARIATIONS

If you have a leadfoot like I do, you'll be stomping on this like you are trying to kick a door down. If that's the case, you'll need a very strong cigar box with a thick lid. (Look for boxes by Undercrown Cigars; they work great.)

I added metal trunk corners to this Undercrown box stomper (see Figure 5-10). It also has rubber feet to keep it from sliding around.

You can also use an old soda crate with a plywood top added, as seen here. This stomper has five different piezos wired throughout the underside and wired to the preamp, which is mounted on top. I added a few metal corner brackets around the preamp to protect it from wear and tear of the road. (These preamps can be fragile. Keep them from getting crushed!) The guitar jack is mounted on the side.

I also added two eyehooks to the back of the box (not shown) for attaching a bungee cord that was wrapped around my stool. This keeps the Foot Stomper from moving anywhere!

I played the Coca Cola crate Foot Stomper (Figure 5-11) for over four years. Notice the wear marks on the thick plywood top. I used salvaged plywood as the stomper top and three internal piezo discs, providing a less-than-suitable response and

Figure 5-10.

Figure 5-11.

requiring Bruce Lee–caliber kicking to get a good sound. A good pair of cowboy boots enhanced the tone.

Since retiring it for a smaller cigar box version, I have plans on converting it into a coffee table!

*Be prepared to fight with your sound guy!* Foot Stompers are not normal instruments and uptight soundmen tend to get bitchy when dealing with them. Insist on having the instrument dialed in with 100% bass, no mids, and treble. He may complain that the stomper is redlining the mixing board. Fight for the "combat boot to the chest" tone. He may whine that there is a hum coming from the primitive electronics. Tell him to put a noise gate on it if he has one.

When dialed in correctly, your stomp becomes a blast that fills the room, turning your music into something very physical to the audience.

*Note: Due to the piezo setup, the Foot Stomper can elicit feedback if positioned too close to stage monitors. Simply move it away from the monitor a bit.*

## One Man Band Playing Technique: Getting into the Groove

Anybody can kick a Foot Stomper, but few people realize that it's just one part of physical performance that requires the choreography of your entire body. Your strumming, singing, and stomping should all be approached like a drummer on a trap set; every movement working in coordination. This means your guitar strumming or soloing

### "The John Henry" Spike and Hammer Stomper

It's the perfect percussion when you want that authentic "Cool Hand Luke" tone!

I got this device from an insane metalworker in Huntsville, AL who goes by the stage name Pete Regan. The device, which I call "The John Henry," was created as a foot percussion unit that emulates chain gangs hammering railroad spikes.

The John Henry features an actual metal hammer welded to a fulcrum that brings it up to smack a railroad spike that was welded to the frame. A section of chain dangles from the hammer, providing an eerie clink as the hammer falls to the ground.

When we recorded my album *Holler!*, we had the goal of creating music based on old field hollers, prison songs, and work chants. The John Henry became an integral part of the sound and was multi-tracked, sometimes up to 12 layers, making the rhythm section sound like a chain gang from the Parchmen Farm Prison or something from *Cool Hand Luke*. There ain't nothin' meaner than prison blues.

must fit into the *entire groove*. A quick YouTube search of Seasick Steve, Ben Prestage, or Richard Johnston will give a good example of one-man grooving.

Your ultimate goal is to get the audience's heads bobbing to the beat. Get that Stomper dialed in to a crushing thud and dig a groove so deep that the entire place falls in. Once the crowd starts bobbing their heads, you now *own them*. They're yours to take for a ride.

# CHAPTER 6: Electric Washtub Bass, a.k.a. "The Soul Bucket"

PHOTO: DAVID SUTTON

Feedback-proof design with a setup that gives 1½ octaves of bass boogie.

If the goal is to deliver bare-knuckle blues to an unsuspecting audience, the Soul Bucket is the muscle behind the knuckles.

It was a cold December night when we showed up to the bar that had the toughest crowds in town. We knew this was going to be a funeral from the start, having dealt with this unresponsive crowd in the past. I thought I could alleviate things by covering the stage in 14 sets of various Christmas lights, all set up to control units that blink to the music. None of it mattered because of one major problem: Farmer Jon was sick and called off, leaving an empty space on stage for him and his "The Soul Bucket," the electric washtub bass.

Without the Soul Bucket, the band sounded like the tinkling of wine glasses, even with the Foot Stomper's thunder.

*If the goal is to deliver bare-knuckle blues to an unsuspecting audience, the Soul Bucket is the muscle behind the knuckles.*

PHOTO: DAVID SUTTON

"The string is essential because it has more stretch than a steel bass string. Any tighter or more rigid and the string won't let you bend the notes in like an upright fretless bass. It's hard to hit notes right out of the blue. You gotta slide up to them."

–Farmer Jon, washtub bassist for Shane Speal & the Snakes

Trash rock requires the thunder of a Soul Bucket electric washtub bass and my band needs Farmer Jon to make it complete. The Soul Bucket may only have one string, but it's the essential earthquake-inducing string. Unlike traditional washtub basses that delivered percussive "whump whump" sounds to jug bands of the past, a Soul Bucket is a musical one-string bass guitar, capable of running bass lines. It growls like a washtub should, but it growls *in tune*!

The key elements that deliver tone are the acoustic pickup internally attached to the eyehook and the 80-gauge weed whacker string. The pickup faithfully amplifies the tones while reducing feedback (even on blaring festival stages when we opened up for Jackyl) and the weed whacker string enables a 1½ octave range. It's a sound you just can't get from the old clothesline washtub basses.

The washtub bass has direct roots in Central and South Africa, related to an instrument called the Ground Harp. This grandfather of the gutbucket looked like an animal trap and consisted of a shallow pit dug beside a tree or next to a flexible stick shoved into the ground, an animal skin stretched and staked over the pit, and a string attached to the middle of the skin and attached to a tree limb. The musician would pull on the branch or stick to change the tension of the string.

The American version of the washtub bass came into prominence in the Spasm Bands of New Orleans in the late 1800s and later in the 1920s and 1930s jug bands of Memphis and Louisville.

This version of the washtub bass, using a feedback-proof pickup design, was developed between Farmer Jon and myself, encompassing several prototypes with the washtub sometimes rewired in the backroom of a local dive bar just to make it work. As with all designs in this book, always pack duct tape in your gig bag, just in case.

Figure 6-1.

## PARTS:
- Standard washtub with the handles removed
- ⅜" (1 cm) eyebolt, 6" (15¼") length with two hex nuts (You may need to buy two eye bolts in order to get two matching nuts)
- Two large washers
- 80-gauge weed whacker string (Farmer Jon buys the cheap stuff from WalMart). Do not use star-shaped string, or it'll rip your fingers up when you play! Get the rounded string.
- Shovel handle
- Acoustic guitar preamp with piezo rod pickup (See page 46)

## TOOLS:
- Drill with ⅜" (1 cm) bit and ⅛" (⅓ cm) bit (Optional: A step drill bit for boring holes into metal)
- Rotary tool with cut-off wheel bit or tin snips
- Electrical tape
- Electronics heat-shrink wrap tubing for ⅜" (1 cm) wire

Drill a ⅜" (1 cm) hole in the washtub (Figure 6-1) while singing "Ain't No Hole in the Wash Tub" by Emmet Otter's Jug Band (the greatest Muppet movie ever). As seen in the photo, I prefer using a step bit to drill into metal. The end result is a cleaner hole requiring less deburring.

Unknown band, circa 1890s.

Figure 6-2.

Preamp hole: Draw a rectangle
1¼" x 3¾" (3 x 9½ cm) on the side for
the preamp. Draw an "X" between the
corners (Figure 6-2).

Cut an "X" from corner to corner
using rotary tool or tin snips. Fold the
triangle portions back into the washtub,
making a perfect little rectangle for the
preamp to be mounted onto inside
(Figure 6-3). You don't need to cut
the triangles out. Just fold them back.
Drill ⅜" (1 cm) hole positioned 4" (10
cm) below the preamp hole for the
guitar jack.

**Eye bolt setup:** Insert a hex nut and
washer onto the eye bolt the entire way
up the shaft (Figure 6-4).

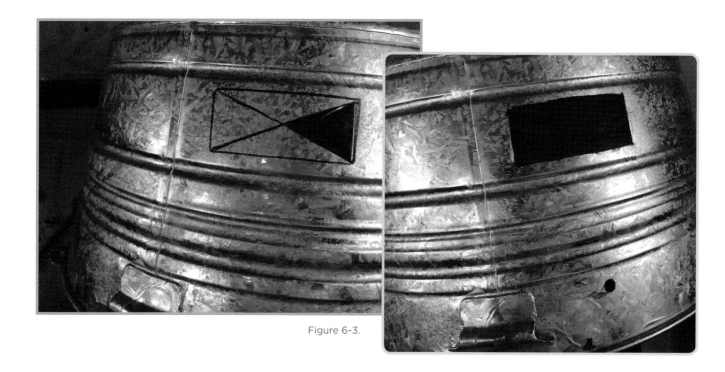

Figure 6-3.

Figure 6-4.

Figure 6-5.

Figure 6-6.

Place the eyebolt into the center hole of the washtub (Figure 6-5).

Turn the tub over and insert the other washer and hex nut onto the eyebolt and tighten (Figure 6-6). This puts the majority of the eyebolt length inside the tub, allowing you to mount the piezo rod pickup onto it from the inside.

Figure 6-7.

Take the piezo rod pickup and place the top pickup-side against the eyebolt with the connecting wire facing the underside of the tub (Figure 6-7).

Using electrical tape, tightly wrap the piezo rod against the eyebolt (Figure 6-8). Make sure the top of the pickup makes full contact with the side of the eyebolt. (This will ensure the transfer of the string vibration from the bolt directly to the pickup.)

Figure 6-8.

Figure 6-9.

Figure 6-10.

Figure 6-11.

Slip shrink-wrap tubing over pickup/bolt assembly and heat to shrink (Figure 6-9). Add extra tape if you think it will come loose.

Install the preamp into the side of the washtub by first drilling small pilot holes for the mounting screws. Also install the guitar jack (Figure 6-10).

Turn the tub back over. Following the preamp instructions, plug the piezo rod pickup into the preamp (Figure 6-11).

Drill an ⅛" (⅓ cm) hole in the top of the shovel handle, about 6" (15¼ cm) from the end (Figure 6-12). This will be the hole for tying the string.

Drill another ⅛" (⅓ cm) hole at the opposite end of the shovel handle (Figure 6-13). Important: Make sure the notch is perpendicular to the ⅛" (⅓ cm) hole you drilled on top. This will place the string facing the center of the washtub.

Using a saw, cut off the end of the stick in the middle of the hole (Figure 6-14).

Figure 6-12.

Figure 6-13.

Figure 6-14.

This will give you a perfect notch at the end of the stick for holding it against the rim of the tub (Figure 6-15).

Place the washtub on the floor and tie the weed whacker string to the eyebolt. Place the groove on the bottom of the shovel handle on the rim of the tub. Point the handle inward so that the top hole is over the eyebolt. Run the length of weed whacker to the top of the handle and tie it to the top (Figure 6-16).

This will give you enough area to pull back and forth (Figure 6-17), delivering a good octave or more of notes.

Figure 6-15.

Figure 6-16.

Figure 6-17.

Farmer Jon and I put the band together literally right on stage during open mic nights that I used to host. He just showed up one night with his Soul Bucket #1 and sat in. On another night, Ronn Benway joined in on washboard and soon, Aaron Lewis joined in on harmonica. Like feeding stray dogs, they kept returning week after week to improvise deep boogie with me. Ronn still sits in with the band from time to time and Aaron has since moved on, but Farmer Jon has been playing with me ever since and is the one constant member in my band.

I'll be honest, for the first two years of playing with these guys I never paid

## Blues Legend, Clarence "Gatemouth" Brown's Washtub Drum and Cigar Box Fiddle

### EXCERPTED FROM *GUITAR PLAYER* MAGAZINE, MAY 1979

"The first set of drums I played cost me a whippin'," he laughs. "I sneaked one of my mom's washtubs out and got me two tree limbs and put 'em to it. Man, I was wailing away, and my mom came out there and tore the tub all to pieces and, of course, she tore me up, too. That was my first encounter with a set of drums. And my first fiddle—I tried to make it out of a cigar box and screen wire, and it didn't work."

attention to Farmer Jon's Soul Bucket playing. Because I'd be playing cigar box guitar and Foot Stomper while singing, I never spent the time to truly listen to his bass. That changed when we recorded our first album, *Holler!* There was a point during the recording process when Farmer Jon had to track his bass parts separately from the rest of the band. As the album's producer, I had to sit in the control room listening to him in fine detail.

Soon, the truth of his playing came out of the speakers. "Holy shit," I screamed. "He's playing running gospel bass lines!" Sure enough, Farmer Jon had developed a style that encompassed in-the-pocket blues, gospel bass, and New Orleans tuba lines. He's the greatest washtub player I've ever heard.

## Playing the Soul Bucket

To start playing the washtub bass, you'll need to position yourself with one foot on the edge of the washtub, keeping it steady on the floor. Place the groove at the end of the shovel handle on the rim to hold it in place and act as a fulcrum. Plug the bass in to a PA system or bass amp and play along with your stereo, practicing the technique of pulling *up* to each note. Remember, it's simple to play the Soul Bucket, but it's difficult to play the Soul Bucket *well*.

Farmer Jon tells me that he's developed muscle memory for where low G, low C, and low E are located. (These are our most common keys in the band.) After he destroyed Bucket #4 during our 2017 Dive Bar Tour, I built him a new one with a slightly longer neck. He said it totally messed with his noting and took him two gigs to get used to the new setup.

As stated above, the instrument also requires you to slide up to the note, giving the distinctive "mwah" sound. Your own playing style will be connected with whomever you jam with on a regular basis.

*Note: Because of the 80-gauge string, the Soul Bucket delivers tones in the baritone range. To really get it low and growling in the low bass range, run the signal through a guitar octave pedal. Start by setting the pedal at one octave down, mixed with the original signal at about 50%. Tweak as needed.*

PHOTO: FREDDIE GRAVES

The Soul Bucket and its master, Farmer Jon.

# CHAPTER 7: Beer Can Microphone

Get an AM radio sound to your singing! Beer can microphones also double as an incredible harmonica mic.

Let's get this out of the way right now: I'm the biggest fraud in the entertainment world because:
- I compose simple songs
- These simple songs are accompanied by my substandard guitar playing
- To top it all off, there's my god-awful singing

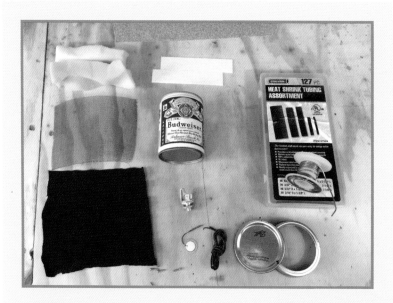

And yet, we still pack a damn bar for an entire three-hour-long concert.

My fans aren't stupid people, nor are they deaf. They're just looking to rock out, sing along, and have fun. We're not there to give a recital; we're there to give a *show*.

But I have several secrets that snag the audience like a fish hook to a large mouth bass:

- My simple songs are fun to sing along. Choruses are memorable—like bumper sticker slogans. Themes like drinkin', killin', and big-legged women.
- My simplistic guitar playing is used on three- and four-string cigar box guitars that look cobbled together, but are solid players. The instruments are as much of a prop to the audience as they are my lifeblood to music.
- My god-awful singing is delivered through a beer can microphone. This homemade device covers a multitude of sins by making my voice sound like it's coming through an AM radio. A touch of slap-back echo added to the PA system rounds out the vocal delivery.

*Because if you can't dazzle them with brilliance, baffle them with bullshit.*

## PARTS:

- Antique steel beer can
- A standard Mason jar lid and insert
- 20 mm round piezo disk with pre-wired leads
- ¼" (⅔ cm) guitar jack
- 20-gauge wire
- Heat shrink tubing
- A scrap piece of soft foam rubber (large enough to fill the inside of the can). Interestingly enough, the foam rubber needed is the same type that is used for clown noses.
- Four small screws, such as #2 ⅜" (1 cm) nickel-plated screws (guitar tuner screws)
- 4" (10 cm) square section of an old T-shirt (Red looks best)
- 4" (10 cm) section of window screen wire
- 6" (15¼ cm) strip of self-stick felt (or 6" (15¼ cm) of self-stick fuzzy side of Velcro®)

## TOOLS:

- Drill with ¹⁄₁₆" (1½ mm) bit and ⅜" (1 cm) bit (Suggested: a stepped drill bit works better than a ⅜" (1 cm) bit)
- Hot glue gun
- Adjustable wrench
- Soldering iron and solder
- Rough sandpaper

Figure 7-1.

The beer can microphone is the simplest instrument in this book. In its most basic form, the mic is nothing but contact mic (in this case, a round piezo element) touching a Mason jar lid. When you sing close to the lid, the metal vibrates the contact mic, which then goes into the PA system.

That's basically it.

This mic design was first shown to me by cigar box guitar builder, Brian Saner. A more refined version was later given to me by rockabilly guitar virtuoso, Jesse Austin. (Thank you both for helping me mask my sickly singing!)

The microphones in these photos were made from older, steel beer cans. Do yourself a favor and seek out steel cans simply because new aluminum cans crush easily. You can find steel beer cans at flea markets, antique stores, and on eBay.

*Note: Beer can collecting became popular in the 1970s and lined many man cave walls. If you keep searching, you can sometimes find entire collections for sale on Craigslist or eBay.*

The Budweiser can in the photo is shorter than a normal 12-oz. (355 ml) can. This is a rarer 8-oz. (237 ml) can (known as "pony cans" in dive bars around here). The Pabst Blue Ribbon can is a long 16-oz. (473 ml) can (known as "pounders" in the dives). The can length has very little to do with the tone. The shorter pony cans are more ergonomic when used as a harmonica mic, allowing the performer to cup them in the hand with the harp. The long pounder cans just look cool on stage. (It's my belief that everything can be a prop on stage if you take the time to plan and build them right. Cool props enhance the concert experience.)

You'll need to remove the lid of the can without damaging the steel ring around the

Figure 7-2.

lip of the can. To do this, simply turn the can upside-down and grind it into a piece of rough sand paper until the lid just pops off from the can (Figure 7-1). You can also use a belt sander if you have one.

Drill a ⅜" (1 cm) hole into the bottom of the can. I prefer a stepped drill bit for a cleaner hole, but a ⅜" (1 cm) bit will work fine, too (Figure 7-2).

Figure 7-3.

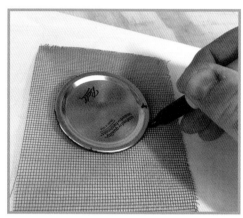

Figure 7-4.

Wiring the piezo disc: Wire the piezo disc to the guitar jack using lengths of 20-gauge wire that are 2" (5 cm) longer than the length of the beer can. Black wire is wired to the ground (inner sleeve) lug and the red to the lead lug (Figure 7-3).

Lay the Mason jar insert on top of the screen wire and draw an outline using a black marker (Figure 7-4). Cut the circle out using tin snips. Make sure to cut on the outside of the circle so it is slightly larger than the lid insert.

Lay the Mason jar insert on top of the T-shirt section. Faintly draw a circle ½" (1¼ cm) wider than the lid. Cut the circle out (Figure 7-5).

Line the beer can lid with self-stick felt (Figure 7-6). This gives the can a snug fit into the Mason jar lid.

Insert the guitar jack inside the base of the can and mount it into the hole (Figure 7-7). Tighten with a wrench.

Figure 7-5.

Figure 7-6.

Figure 7-7.

Figure 7-8.

Figure 7-9.

Figure 7-10.

Figure 7-11.

Turn the Mason lid insert over and sand a quarter-sized spot on the underside, exposing the metal (Figure 7-8).

Using a hot glue gun, glue the metal side of the piezo disc to the lid insert (Figure 7-9).

Gently insert the foam rubber into the can so that it isn't smashed inside. Mark the foam ½" (1¼ cm) above the top of the can (Figure 7-10). Pull it out, cut it at the mark, and then reinsert (Figure 7-11).

Place the cloth and screen wire on top of the lid (Figure 7-12). (The lid is underneath the shirt material and hidden in the picture.) Press the insert into the Mason lid (Figure 7-13). It should fit snugly inside.

Place the Mason jar lid on the beer can, keeping slight pressure on the lid so that it's touching the top of the can. Drill four small pilot holes around the edge with a ⅛" (½ cm) bit. Insert the small screws into the holes (Figure 7-14).

The mic is complete and ready to be tested (Figure 7-15). Beware: These microphones are lo-fi weapons and feedback is always lurking

Figure 7-12.

Figure 7-13.

Figure 7-14.

around the corner. You'll need to position them away from your monitors and PA speakers. (It's worth the effort!)

Using a guitar cord, plug it into a guitar amp or PA system. When singing into the mic, place your mouth very close to the top. For best results, plug the mic into the standalone preamp shown in chapter 10 (page 142) and then into a PA system or guitar amp. Dial in mostly midrange on the preamp for a convincing "squashed" AM radio tone.

## Tuning the Mic

The scrap of foam rubber places pressure against the Mason jar lid, keeping the piezo element from excessive feedback. If the foam rubber is too long and puts excessive pressure on the lid, the mic will be quieter. Take the screws out of the top and push the foam down a little (or trim a bit of foam off the top). If the foam hardly touches the lid, then the mic will sound "woofy" and lose clarity, making your voice sound like you're talking into a blanket. If that happens, take the mic apart and add a small piece of scrap foam on top.

Figure 7-15.

## BEER CAN MIC PHOTO GALLERY

Olde Frothingslosh Beer was another Pittsburgh beer, originally created as a joke by a local radio DJ and later brought to life by a brewery. The can, featuring a voluptuous Miss Frothingslosh, is the perfect thing to make a mic for singing blues about "big leg wimmins."

A 1976 Iron City Beer can features the Pittsburgh Steelers. I came across a dozen of these cans and turned them into microphones. Every single one of them sold within two days at a music festival near Pittsburgh.

Two more classic beer cans, turned into mics. Rusty cans like the Miller High Life add a great look.

## Other Lo-Fi Vocal Effects

There's a million ways of destroying your vocal tones and I've tried them all. On my first album, *Jug Fusion*, I sang the chorus of "Jesus Is Comin' Soon" into a telephone that was connected to an intercom inside the recording studio control room. I've also sung through Radio Shack megaphones and toy megaphones made to be mounted on kids' bicycles. I've even sung into foam cups with the bottoms ripped out, a technique stolen from the 1966 Top 40 hit "Winchester Cathedral" by the New Vaudeville Band.

Poor man's tone in a rich man's package: This is my crusty Copperphone microphone by Placid Audio that I've used in concert and on record to achieve lo-fi tones. The mic is handmade by Mark Pirro, bassist for the bands Tripping Daisy and Polyphonic Spree. Legend has it that Pirro harnessed the secrets of Cold War military-grade communication elements to create these beasts. They're used in studios worldwide by some of the biggest names in music.

My Copperphone comes in handy when a beer can mic can't handle louder stage volumes. It's also an incredible tool in the recording studio for making vocals and instruments sound like they were recorded in the 1930s.

When I first received this mic, it was wonderfully shiny and polished. After eight years of use, it's now scratched, caked with grime, and smells like beer and tobacco.

# CHAPTER 8: 2 x 4 Lap Steel Guitar

I was sitting in the booth of a Waffle House in Huntsville, Alabama, starting at my coffee and trying to work through a gig hangover.

*Gig hangover: The morning after a show that consists of a pounding headache, sore muscles, bruises, scrapes, back pain, ringing ears . . . and the major desire to get out there and do it all over again.*

I had 18 hours of driving ahead of me to get back to Pennsylvania after playing a fantastic, yet physically draining, cigar box guitar festival. I crouched in the booth seat, ears still ringing, trying to give my mind respite from anything related to homemade instruments.

## PARTS:

- 32" (81 cm) section of 2 x 4 (38 x 89 mm) pine lumber (Note: Due to harmful chemicals, do not use pressure-treated lumber!)
- Two 2" x ¾" (5 x 2 cm) metal corner brackets (Find these in the cabinetmaking section of the hardware store)
- One pack of guitar tuners, three per side
- Cheap single coil pickup. For this, I used a P90 "Soapbar" pickup from *CBGitty.com*. Similar pickups can also be found by searching "Lap Steel Soap Bar Pickup" on eBay and Amazon. The plans are tailored toward this pickup, but you could easily notch out the route for an almost any single coil guitar pickup.
- ¼" (⅔ cm) guitar jack
- Strat-style jack plate
- 24 black plastic zip ties, 14" (35½ cm) length
- Pack of medium-gauge electric guitar strings

## TOOLS:

- Electric drill and two drill bits: ³⁄₃₂" (¼ cm) and ⅝" (1½ cm)
- Table saw or circular saw
- Small screwdriver
- Hacksaw, metal file, or rotary tool
- Soldering iron and solder
- Wire stripper or cutter
- Wood screws, paint, or black permanent marker

But then Hank Williams' "Cold Cold Heart" crept out of the jukebox.

Ah . . . "Cold Cold Heart." It starts with Don Helms' aching, desperate steel guitar that jumps out of the speakers and pierces your soul. Damn, there's nothing like hearing Hank Williams' steel guitar while recovering in an Alabama greasy spoon. I knew I had to make my own lap steel guitar when I got back home, just to preserve this feeling. Fortunately, I had an 18-hour drive ahead to plan this out.

This is one of the easiest homemade guitars I have ever built and it only took me an afternoon to make. This lap steel was made from an extra 2 x 4 (38 x 89 mm) I had in my shed and it just required a few saw cuts to the wood.

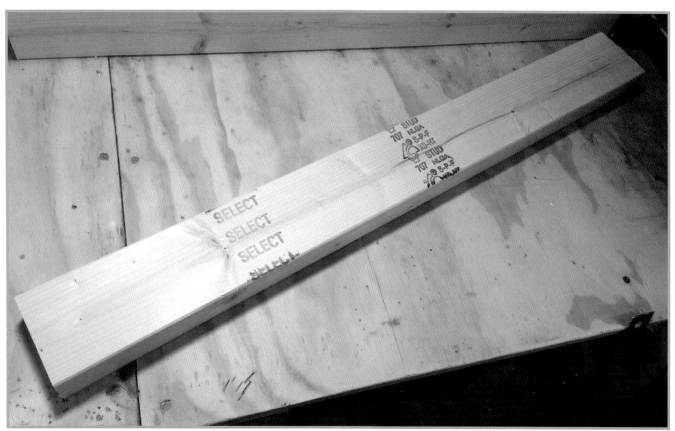

Figure 8-1.

The lap steel plays great, too. It's set up with a standard 23" (58½ cm) scale, just like the store bought lap steels! The whole thing feels great on your lap and looks absurdly cool.

These plans will give you a very basic, yet absolutely playable lap steel. You are just marking down a few lines, making a couple cuts to the 2 x 4 (38 x 89 mm) and installing simple hardware.

Cut a standard pine 2 x 4 (38 x 89 mm) into a 32" (81 cm) length (Figure 8-1).

Mark the headstock cutaway by turning the 2 x 4 (38 x 89 mm) on its side and mark a vertical line 4" (10 cm) from the left end. Mark a horizontal line ⅝" (1½ cm) from the top (as pictured, Figure 8-2).

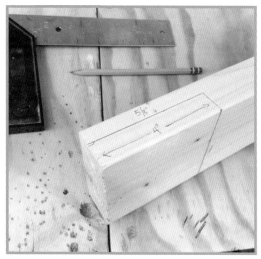

Figure 8-2.

Figure 8-3.

Notch out the bottom portion in the headstock area. Just like the cigar box guitar project, I use my table saw to notch out the area by cutting multiple passes (Figure 8-3). You can also use wood files, hand saws, or a band saw.

Turn the 2 x 4 (38 x 89 mm) back over and the following marks on the board (Figure 8-4), starting from the butt end and going up toward the headstock:

a) 1½" (3¾ cm) (this will be our through-body string feed)

b) 3" (7½ cm) (bridge location and beginning of pickup cavity)

c) 4½" (11½ cm) (end of pickup cavity)

d) 26" (66 cm) (nut location)

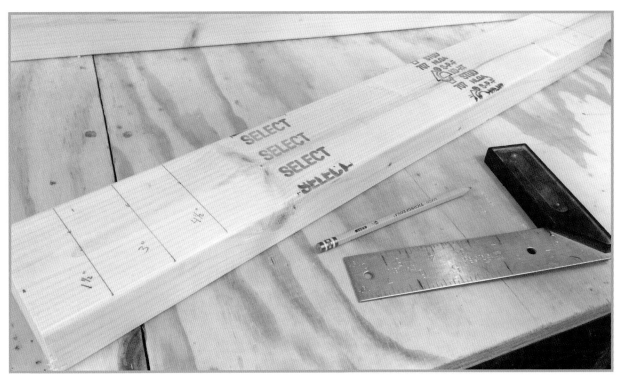

Figure 8-4.

Figure 8-5.

Figure 8-6.

Cut out the pickup cavity: Notch out the wood between the 3" (7½ cm) and 4½" (11½ cm) line. Go about ¼" (⅔ cm) deep. Use the same notching technique as above with the headstock. Drill the string feed holes across the 1½" (3¾ cm) line (Figure 8-5). Use a 3⁄32" (¼ cm) drill bit to drill six holes 3⁄8" (1 cm) apart for the strings to feed through the body. Drill through the depth of the 2 x 4 (38 x 89 mm).

Drill tuner holes (Figure 8-6): Mark the tuner holes on the underside of the headstock. Go in about 5⁄8" (1½ cm) in on each side and space the tuners roughly an inch apart. Use a 5⁄8" (1½ cm) drill bit to drill the tuner holes.

Figure 8-7.

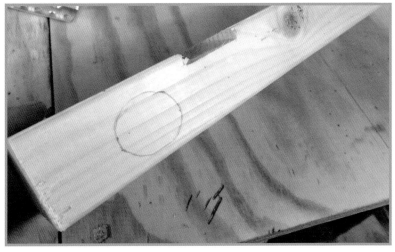

Figure 8-8.

Place the corner brackets together and use small clamps or clothespins to hold them together (Figure 8-7). Mark six string notches, each ⅜" (1 cm) apart, on the tops of the brackets. Using a hacksaw, metal file, or a rotary tool with a cut-off bit, cut six string notches into the metal corners. Go down about ⅛" (⅓ cm) deep. Clean up any metal burrs and file down any sharp corners.

Route out a guitar jack cavity: Starting 1¼" (3 cm) from the end of the 2 x 4 (38 x 89 mm), draw an oval that is about 1½" (3¾ cm) wide, as shown (Figure 8-8). Using a ¾" (2 cm) Forstner bit, rotary tool, or chisel,

Figure 8-9.

route out the area to a depth of ¾" (2 cm) deep (Figure 8-9).

To check the depth of your guitar jack route, take the ¼" (⅔ cm) guitar jack and insert it *backward* into the Strat-style jack plate, as shown (Figure 8-10). Install the washer and nut and tighten with a wrench. Place the assembly over the pickup route and make sure the guitar jack lugs don't touch any wood. If so, cut the route deeper. Sand any rough edges on the lap steel. If you plan on painting or adding polyurethane, do it now. I skipped all finish work on this lap steel and kept the raw look, including the "STUD" stamping.

Figure 8-10.

Figure 8-11.

Figure 8-12.

Drill a channel between the pickup route and the jack route using a ³⁄₁₆" (½ cm) drill bit (Figure 8-11). Install the tuner bushings and tuners (Figure 8-12).

Mark your fret guides (Figure 8-13): Using the same 23" (58½ cm) fretboard guide on page 173, measure out the frets by starting at the 26" (66 cm) nut location and making pencil marks for each fret location. Then use a contractor's square to draw the fret lines.

Installing the metal corner nut and bridge: Center and install the first metal corner (serving as the nut) at the first fret line, making sure the cut grooves are facing up. The screw anchors should point toward the tuners as shown (Figure 8-14). Center and install the second metal corner at the beginning of the pickup route with the screw anchors, pointing toward the string holes as shown (Figure 8-15).

Feed the pickup wires through the channel and mount the pickup using the two mounting screws (Figure 8-16).

Figure 8-13.

Figure 8-14.

Figure 8-15.

Figure 8-16.

Figure 8-17.

Figure 8-18.

Figure 8-19.

Figure 8-20.

Cut the pickup wire 2½" (6⅓ cm) from the 2 x 4 (38 x 89 mm) (Figure 8-17). Strip the outer insulation, revealing the lead wire and ground wires. Wrap the ground wires together. Strip ¼" (⅔ cm) of insulation off of the lead wire (Figure 8-18). Save the leftover wire.

Solder the ground wire to the lug attached to the inner sleeve of the guitar jack and the lead wire to the remaining lug (Figure 8-19). Install the guitar jack plate to the side of the 2 x 4 (38 x 89 mm), as shown (Figure 8-20).

"Poor Man's Pickup Ground Wire" – Using the leftover wire from above, pull out the small lead wire and cut a 2½" (6⅓ cm) section from it. Strip ¼" (⅔ cm) from each end and attach one end to the back screw of the jack plate. Attach the other side to the closest bridge screw. To attach the wire, simply unscrew the screw several turns, wrap the wire around the screw, and then screw it back into place (Figure 8-21).

Figure 8-21.

Figure 8-22.

Figure 8-23.

Figure 8-24.

Figure 8-25.

Wrap the black zip ties around each fret mark on the fretboard. Pull them tight, straighten them out and then cut off the excess with scissors (Figure 8-22).

Optional: Add fret dot markers using short wood screws, paint, or even a Sharpie® marker. Position them at the 3, 5, 7, 9, 12, 15, 17, 19, 21, 24 frets (Figure 8-23).

String up the lap steel, but leave the strings slackened (Figure 8-24). If the string ball ends start to pull through the soft pinewood, place a small nail through the ball loop of the string to keep it anchored. Another alternative is to place small washers on each string, anchoring the ball ends to the rear of the lap steel.

Tighten the strings up (Figure 8-25). If they pull out of the nut or bridge notches, remove the strings and cut the notches deeper.

## Tune the Guitar Up

Try an open D chord to start (D, A, D, F#, A, D low to high). This is a blues-based tuning and serves as a great starting place for beginner lap steel players.

Other tunings to try with this string arrangement (all charted low to high):
Open G: G, B, D, G, B, D
Hawaiian A: E, A, E, A, C#, E
Open G (low bass): D, G, D, G, B, D

A quick YouTube search for "How to Play Lap Steel Guitar" will give you more info than you can learn in a lifetime.

## Choosing a Slide for Your Lap Steel

A lap steel slide (called a "tone bar") needs to span the width of all six strings and extend a little over each side. This will enable you to eventually do advanced slant-bar moves.

Many commercial-tone bars are available, but if you want to keep things DIY, try using a deep well socket or a T-shaped copper pipe connector.

## Extra: The Mythical Truckstop Tuning

But wait . . . if you want the mythical truck stop sound as heard into Hank Williams's "Cold Cold Heart," you'll need to change the strings and tune it differently. Don Helms's lap steel guitar was tuned to the classic Nashville C6 tuning. To accomplish this, need a pack of C6 Lap Steel guitar strings— or you can make your own pack using the following string gauges:
#6 (lowest string) – .034 gauge Nickel Wound
#5 – .030 gauge Nickel Wound
#4 – .024 gauge Nickel Wound
#3 – .020 gauge Nickel Wound
#2 – .017 gauge Plain Steel
#1 (highest string) – .014 gauge Plain Steel

Tune the guitar C-E-G-A-C-E, low to high and then search YouTube for "How to Play C6 Lap Steel Tuning." But beware: you must approach C6 with caution. Once you retune to the legendary tuning, you'll never go back. It'll suck you into a world of tears in beers, Patsy Cline going crazy, and make you want to buy a ten-gallon hat to go with your tooled leather chaps. I warned ya.

## Modding Your 2 x 4 Lap Steel

This is wildest 2 x 4 (38 x 89 mm) lap steel ever (see Figure 8-26). It started its life just like the instrument described above. The psychedelic paint job was based on John Lennon's acoustic guitar from the Magical Mystery Tour era. After spray-painting the 2 x 4 (38 x 89 mm) in teal, I taped off the wavy lines and spray painted a darker blue over top. The paint job was finished with some pin striping on the lines using a black paint marker.

Instead of using zip ties, I cut a piece of Plexiglas® to fit the fretboard area and hand painted the lines on the underside. Once dry, I screwed it to the face of the instrument.

After completing the lap steel, I went to the hardware store and purchased three

Figure 8-26.

Figure 8-27.

tapered table legs with mounting brackets and arranged them in a tripod on the underside. It was a perfect finish to a freaky instrument.

The Plexiglas fret board idea inspired me to try other crazy colors, especially glitter spray paint from the craft store (see Figure 8-27).

This teal 2 x 4 (38 x 89 mm) lap steel (Figure 8-28) sparkles in the light and is an awesome prop on stage (it sounds kickass, too). After crafting my own Plexiglas® fret boards on the early prototypes, the folks over at *CBGitty.com* honored my request to make laser-cut clear fretboards for 2 x 4s (38 x 89 mm) in their New Hampshire workshop. (Thanks, Gitty gang!)

The clear fret boards inspired me to use them as a picture frame, much in the same way my grandmother put my school pictures under the glass top of her coffee table. In this example (Figure 8-29), I used a Mardi Gras poster section by New Orleans icon, Amzie Adams.

The pearl and girlie-look (see Figure 8-30) was achieved by sandwiching a strip of pearloid drum wrap (salvaged from an old drum set) and a hand-cut girlie print from an old calendar. The girl was held in place on to the pearloid drum wrap with double-sided tape and the whole assembly was attached to the 2 x 4 (38 x 89 mm) with small screws.

Figure 8-28.

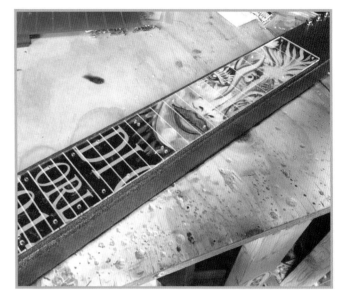

Figure 8-29.

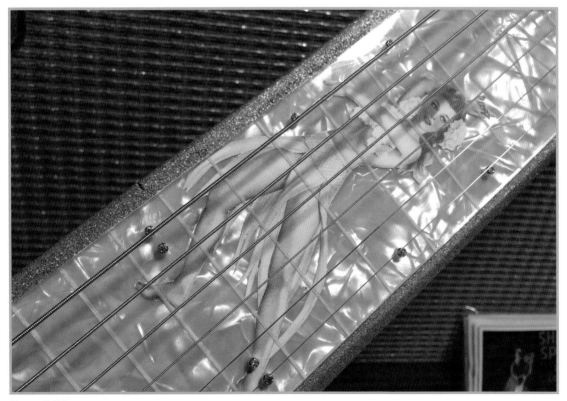

Figure 8-30.

### Unusual Homemade Plywood Guitars (unknown builders) — From the Shane Speal Collection

In the photo on the opposite page, the square four-string baritone guitar on the left was found at a yard sale somewhere in Indiana. The neck is crafted from a thick piece of molding and is strung left handed with E, A, D, G acoustic guitar strings. The body is crafted from ¼" (⅔ cm) plywood and has a nice, loud tone. The high action and fretless neck makes this a slide-only guitar. It was probably built within the last 20 years or so.

The six-string acoustic guitar was built sometime in the 1960s and comes from the Appalachian Mountains. It also has a plywood body and hand-carved neck. The builder spent a lot of time crafting a very playable fretted instrument. A floating bridge, tailpiece, and tuners were salvaged from another guitar.

Poor man's strings: This guitar (left) is still strung with a repaired guitar string. The original owner must have snapped the low E string at the tuner, so he took a section of a wound A string to serve as a "transplant." After all these years, the repair still maintains proper string tension.

## Guitarcheology: Antique One-String Cigar Box "Knee Fiddles" and Their Vaudeville History

PHOTO: RJ GIBSON PHOTOGRAPHY, GETTYSBURG PA

Although this antique-looking photo was just taken a couple years ago, the one-string cigar box guitar in my hands is actually more than 100 years old. This instrument is the centerpiece of my Cigar Box Guitar Museum at Speal's Tavern.

Blues fans always create a hush and reverence paid to antique cigar box guitars that were made with only one string. After all, Blind Willie Johnson learned how to play slide guitar on a one-string cigar box guitar made by his father. Countless other blues legends got their start by making diddley bows, primitive one-string slide guitars which were nothing but old broom wire nailed to a barn wall, held up with bricks and played with a bottle.

Known as the legendary mythical diddley bow, it's the ultimate primitive blues axe and the reason for instruments like this one-string guitar fetching $700 USD or more on eBay.

As I started collecting antique cigar box guitars in my lifelong study, I noticed that most of these one-string cigar box guitars had similar neck lengths (usually 36" [91½ cm] or so) and similar setups. They were also being found in some very non-Delta Blues areas of the US, especially the northeast. There had to be more to the story than just mythical diddley bow slide guitars being built simultaneously.

The answer came from a very different musical source: Vaudeville theater from the early 1900s.

Lee Moran, like many Vaudeville stars, performed skits using a one-string cigar box violin. These instruments usually featured an overall neck length of 32" (81 cm) to 36" (91½ cm), which allowed the instrument to be held between the knees and played like a cello.

As a musician who digs into the past to find his music, this was just the side street I

PHOTO COURTESY OF WILLIAM J. JEHLE COLLECTION. ORIGINALLY PUBLISHED JEHLE'S BOOK, ONE MAN'S TRASH: A HISTORY OF THE CIGAR BOX GUITAR

**Shown:** Vaudevillian, Lee Moran, 1921.

Unidentified child playing a one-string cello, circa 1930s.

needed to take me away from the blues for a while. This is where things get interesting.

At the turn of the twentieth century, Vaudeville was known for the revues, skits, and one-act sketches. One of the favorite gimmicks used by performers was a jug band style music played on one-string cigar box fiddles, rubber hose horns, and other homemade instruments.

Yes, the one-string fiddle started out as a prop for comedy! Before joining the *Three Stooges*, Larry Fine would use his classical violin training to perform outrageous pieces on a one-string cigar box fiddle. Actor W.C. Fields even used his old one-stringer in a scene from the 1936 movie *Poppy*. These things were on stages everywhere.

## Guitarcheology: Antique One-String Cigar Box "Knee Fiddles" and Their Vaudeville History (Continued)

Irby put bow to fiddlestring, waited for the signal. Then he began to play, with his eyes on Billiam.

This is a fine example of a one-string fiddle, pictured (opposite page) beside the book and 78rpm record of *One-String Fiddle* by Erick Berry. The instrument, also known as a "knee fiddle," circa 1940s, was found on eBay. It features a stick-through-box design, just like the cigar box guitar in Chapter 2 (pages 15–45). The fiddle has a dowel rod tuner and a piece of chain link through the middle as a tuning peg.

The book and record are from 1939 and tell the story of Irby and his homemade cigar box fiddle. The inside illustration (left) shows how to hold a "knee fiddle."

Many years back, I got an email from folk singer Fiddlin' Lew Sellinger. He gave me the history of his uncle, a one-string performer in the New York Yiddish Vaudeville scene named Charlie Sellinger. He said his uncle called the instrument a "Broomalin" because the neck was made with a broom handle. He was so well versed on it he could make the instrument cry like a gorgeous soprano and sound like a human voice! In addition to playing the one-string Broomalin, Charlie Sellinger

## Circus One-String Cigar Box Fiddle Story – Henry Wood, 1940s

**FROM *A SAWDUST HEART: MY VAUDEVILLE LIFE IN MEDICINE AND TENT SHOWS* BY HENRY WOOD, AS TOLD TO MICHAEL FEDO: *UNIV OF MINNESOTA PRESS*; 1 EDITION (APRIL 21, 2011)**

Henry Wood was a performer in the famous WLS Barn Dance in Wisconsin back in the 1940s. As master at the musical saw, Wood went on to describe the act he created for the Barn Dance:

*Sometimes Mr. Statz would tell the audience that I'd taken over everything in the barn—cowbells, pitchforks, tin cans, milk pails, saws, and chains to make music with, and there were no tools left for work. He said he fixed me. He'd lock them all up.*

*Well, I'd go into the audience and see if anybody had a cigar box. We'd have a plant there who did, and I'd borrow the box and cut a hole in the top. I'd get a broom handle and attach it, then string a wire across the whole. I'd snatch a violin bow from one of the fellows in the band, and I'd play that one-string fiddle while Mr. Statz would try to make his announcements.*

*It always brought down the house, or more accurately, the tent or barn. When he'd grab my fiddle and break it, the band would start in and I'd still have the stage, doing a comic jig or buck-and-wing dance.*

## Guitarcheology - Antique One-String Cigar Box "Knee Fiddles" and Their Vaudeville History (Continued)

**Stevens Point Daily Journal**

STEVENS POINT, WISCONSIN.

MONDAY, JUNE 15, 1914

Vaudeville Attraction at Grand Saturday and Sunday.

Karl, "The Wizard of the one string", brings forth remarkable tones from his cigar box "fiddle" and the audience couldn't help becoming good natured while he entertained them musically and with his rapid fire talking. Gangler's dog almost talked; in fact they did

**BENEFIT DANCE FOR ARMY BAND**

FITCHBURG DAILY SENTINEL.

WEDNESDAY, APRIL 24, 1918.

Mr. Satz has been on the Keith circuit and also appeared at the Bijou theater a few years ago. He is one of the first to play the trench fiddle, a single string on a cigar box, and is a good singer and clever entertainer.

LANCASTER DAILY EAGLE

Lancaster OH. Mar 23, 1917

Mr. Davis also played some hymns on his one stringed fiddle made from a cigar box and a three cent string, first at one church and then at the other.

also played musical saw and a rubber hose "flexatone" trumpet of his own design.

As the twentieth century rolled along, the one-string fiddle tradition managed to escape the fading Vaudeville stage and grow in popularity via newspaper articles. Stories were penned about local one-string fiddle performers who gave special concerts at churches and special events. A few syndicated newspaper writers started publishing plans on how to make your own. The popularity of these published plans gives a better look at why many of the surviving antique one-string fiddles had similar qualities.

# CHAPTER 9:
## The Mailbox Guitar (A Builder's Diary)

PHOTO: RANDY FLAUM

PHOTO: RANDY FLAUM

PHOTO: RANDY FLAUM

*Desperation inspired, B. B. King baptized*

Back in 1998, I was in the lowest point of my life; my woman had left me and my job hardly paid the bills. I was living in a tiny apartment above a vacuum repair shop with no TV, no Internet, and no one around. All I had was my music collection and a desire to play like my heroes. One particular weekend, I found myself desperately wanting a metal-bodied Dobro guitar so I could play slide guitar blues like Son House.

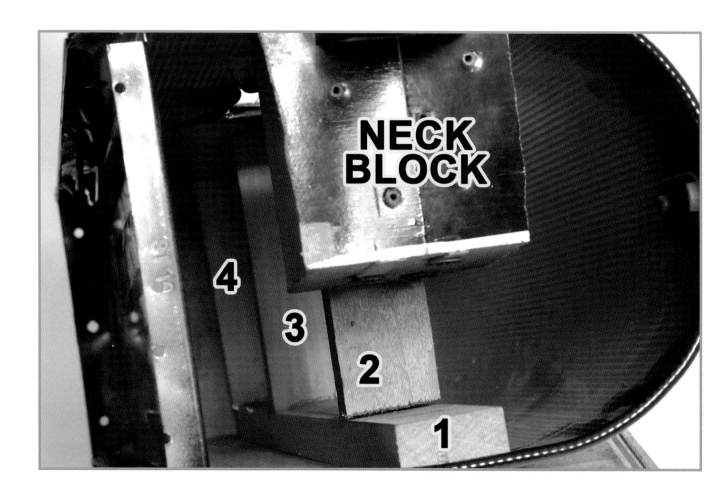

It was 2 a.m. on a Saturday night when I found myself wide-awake with nothing to do and $15 in my pocket. I decided to go to Walmart, the one place in town that was open 24 hours, and find materials that I could use to build an instrument using my cash in hand. After trolling around the empty store, I walked past a cheap metal mailbox in the hardware area and the voice inside my head screamed, "There's my Dobro!" It was $12 on sale, so I grabbed it and made a beeline for the counter.

The next morning, I sacrificed an old Kay acoustic guitar I owned. It was the perfect corpse to extract parts: bolt-on neck, floating bridge, and trapeze tailpiece. Within four hours, the mailbox guitar was complete. It was perfect. It sounded just like a metal-bodied Dobro and it was mine!

After 20 years, this guitar still plays and sounds fantastic. It's been used on many of my albums and has appeared in my concerts.

The following steps aren't exact instructions to build your own Mailbox Guitar. They simply show my improvised building method to make this unique instrument. Sometimes there isn't an exact science to making a poor man's guitar. You just have be an engineer and make it up as you go along.

## BRACING

A look inside the Mailbox Dobro reveals an extremely simple bracing system made from poplar scraps. The wood was left over from some cigar box guitars I was building and served as the perfect primitive material.

Here's a rundown of the bracing system:

1. Body brace – A 1" x 2" (2½ x 5 cm) piece of poplar runs the entire distance of the mailbox along the back. It is secured simply with sheet metal screws.
2. Neck block brace – Sits next to the neck block that was taken from the old Kay guitar. It's glued to the bottom brace and screwed in from the top of the mailbox.
3. Bridge brace – Placed directly underneath the area where the floating bridge would go. Again, it's glued to the bottom and screwed in from the top.
4. Butt brace – Placed at the very rear of the guitar and glued to the bottom brace with additional glue against the back of the mailbox. It's screwed in from the top and back of the mailbox. The trapeze tailpiece is screwed into this brace.

I really should have placed another brace between the neck block and the back brace for better stability. Oh well . . . the guitar has still played fine for the past 17 years.

## NECK BLOCK

I cut, hacked, and ripped out the neck block from the old Kay guitar. I originally thought I could just bolt the neck itself to the mailbox, but I was wrong.

As you can see, the neck block is wider than the neck. This enabled me to run a few sheet metal screws from the top of the mailbox into the top of the neck block.

## COMPONENTS AND TOP OF GUITAR

The guitar's main components came from an old Kay acoustic guitar that was nearly dead. The Kay had a bolt-on neck that I originally thought I could just screw to the mailbox. After some trial and error, I found that I also needed to cut out the entire neck block.

What made the Kay acoustic a perfect candidate for this build was the floating bridge and trapeze tailpiece. (A standard acoustic guitar has a bridge that is glued to the top and wouldn't have worked on this project.) These features meant that I could just add them to the mailbox "body" and, with sufficient bracing, had a working guitar.

Here are the next steps in the process:

1. I used a rotary tool with a cutoff bit to cut a rectangle "neck pocket" into the top of the mailbox. I was able to connect the top of the mailbox with the "wings" of the internal neck block because I used the entire neck block from the Kay guitar, which was wider than the top of the neck.
2. Using the same method as the preamp hole cut into the washtub bass, I used the cutoff wheel to carve a big "X" where the sound hole would be. I then bent back each section of the "X" to reveal a square sound hole that contained no sharp edges.
3. As mentioned above, I used sheet metal screws to hold the internal bridge bracing. This left the screw heads exposed right where the floating bridge would go. I had to use my rotary tool routing bit to remove a little wood from the bottom of the floating bridge to get around the screw heads.

PHOTO:RANDY FLAUM

## TAILPIECE

The trapeze tailpiece has one screw that goes through the mailbox and into the rear brace. Simple. Effective.

The modded Gold Foil pickup (see Chapter 3, pages 62–66) was added several years later. The exposed wire runs through one of the mailbox post mounting holes and into a guitar jack. I placed the pickup in the neck position to give better bass response for this instrument that possessed a boatload of tinny treble.

Oh, and one more secret: The flag was originally made to go on the opposite side of the mailbox. I, of course, placed it prominently on the front of the guitar because, why the hell not?

The amount of string tension started to warp the door of the mailbox, so I added a small block of poplar to the base of the door.

ONE MORE DETAIL: About a year after I created this, I had a chance to meet B. B. King after a concert, and I had him autograph the Mailbox Guitar. Of course, I had him sign the door so it looked like I stole his mailbox and made a guitar out of it. I think I freaked the blues legend out that night.

Remember, if you're gonna freak someone out, might as well do it to the King of the Blues.

## Guitarcheology: Recreating Gus Canon's Banjo (A Builder's Diary by Jim Morris)

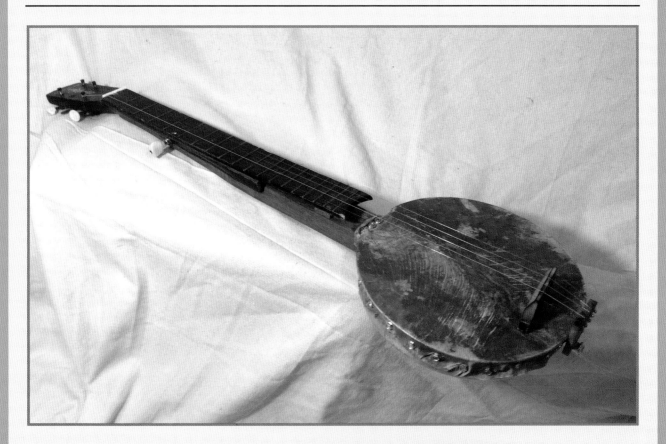

In the small pantheon of jug band legends, Gus Cannon is king. Cannon was one of the very first innovators in jug band music, leading his band, Cannon's Jug Stompers, in the 1920s and 1930s. They delivered wild, driving blues with banjos, jugs, guitars, and more.

It should be noted that Gus Cannon was also the first performer to ever play slide banjo on record. He used a butter knife as a slide on the 1927 recording "Poor Boy, Long Ways from Home."

One evening as I was reading about Cannon and others in the seminal blues history book, *The Country Blues* by Samuel B. Charters, my heart nearly skipped a beat when Charters described Cannon's very first instrument, a homemade banjo:

*He loved music and wanted to learn how to play the banjo, so he made himself one out of a bread pan that his mother gave him and a guitar neck. He put the guitar neck through holes in the side of the dough pan, then covered the pan with a raccoon skin, scraped thin.*

## Guitarcheology: Recreating Gus Canon's Banjo (Continued)

*A lot of country boys made their own banjos this way. The only unsatisfactory aspect was that there were no elaborate drumhead arrangements, with bolts and screws to keep the skin head tight in damp weather. Cannon always traveled with his pockets full of crumpled newspaper, and before he was going to play, he would make a fire with the paper and hold the banjo over the heat until the head was tight enough to play.*

One of the greatest thrills of mixing instrument building, history, and playing is to recreate a guitar from the past using the firsthand accounts found in interviews, plus any other clues that can be dug up. At the time I discovered Gus Cannon's story, I was in the recording studio working on an album, too busy to get in my woodshop. Instead of letting the idea go, I posted a challenge on *www.CigarBoxNation.com* for anybody to recreate Gus' banjo. It was immediately accepted by Jim Morris of Springfield, West Virginia. Morris took my challenge and brought the banjo to life, using the above description along with some other information he had on Gus Cannon. Here are Jim Morris's notes on the instrument:

*Several other sources state that he made the banjo from either a frying pan or a bedpan with the coon skin stretched on it. Either of those would most likely be round and I'm guessing he told the story, or it got re-told, a little differently each time. Either way I'm curious to see what builds come from this! I'm going with frying pan and skin of undisclosed animal since that's what I have on hand.*

*Charter's book says Gus used a bread pan for his first banjo. Other sources say a bedpan and Wikipedia says frying pan. This is what I used.*

*I cut the handle off a frying pan with a hacksaw and that gave me an opening for the neck extension.*

*The animal skin is not raccoon but it was given to me by a friend who's an avid trapper. Suffice to say it's a mammal of some type.*

*I'm not sure what method Gus would've used to attach the skin. I went with self-tapping screws.*

*The neck [is] from a Harmony Caribbean acoustic guitar. I hope I didn't sacrifice a neck that's worth a ton of money to collectors.*

*Note: Morris used a plank of wood as a neck-through mount in which to attach the old Harmony neck. He skillfully carved the wood to a taper that ends at the headstock.*

Soon after he completed the banjo, I had a chance to meet up with Jim Morris at a cigar box guitar festival where he promptly gave me the banjo. It plays phenomenally and truly sounds like something from the early part of the twentieth century. See a video of Jim Morris playing Gus Cannon's "Minglewood Blues" at *www.PoorMansGuitar.com*.

## Antique Ham Can Instruments from the Shane Speal Collection

Neither of these antique instruments are playable. Both feature lids that were soldered back to the can, telling me they were probably made by grownups as toys for kids. The longer instrument has a 20" (51 cm) neck and is strung with four picture-hanging wires, screwed at each end and dangling loosely. The smaller instrument has four pieces of nylon string held in place with eyehooks and screws.

Although these ham can guitars have little historical value, I had to add them to my collection because they remind me of a phone call I got from a rock star many years ago.

It was after 11 p.m. on a hot summer night in 1998 when the phone rang and woke me up. "Shane, I got an idea for you!" said a voice with an excited Southern drawl. "What if you built me a mandolin made out of a *ham can* and electrified it? I'd play it in concert." It was Allen Woody, the bassist for the Allman Brothers and Gov't Mule, on the phone again. Back in the day, Woody would call me up with wild instrument designs and ask if I could make them for him.

"Find a way to put a neck through the ham can, add some frets and I'll send you a pickup from one of my basses to sink in it," he said.

I mumbled some kind of affirmative and told him I would be on the lookout for an old-fashioned metal ham can.

I never did get to make that mandolin for Woody. When I received the call that he passed away on August 26, 2000, I had only collected the pickup, tuners, and fretboard. Life got in the way.

In the months that followed, I searched the Internet for all things Allen Woody, remembering the kind musician who took the time to hang out with me, call me on the

Warren Haynes, Matt Abts, and Allen Woody of Gov't Mule in 1996, holding their new Shane Speal cigar box guitars. I met them at their hotel before a show and gifted them with the instruments. After that day, I would receive many phone calls from Allen Woody requesting weirder and wilder instruments.

phone, and put me on his guest list at concerts. What I found was dozens of other instrument makers with similar stories about late night phone calls, bizarre instrument requests, and the biggest list of endorsements I had ever seen!

So these two antique ham can instruments (on opposite page) reside in my collection as a tribute to Allen Woody. They make me smile when I look at them. They also remind me that I still need to make a ham can mandolin just so I know how one would sound.

This is a two-string bass I built for Allen Woody back in 1996. The body is an old Riunite Wine gift box. It's string with two bass strings on a fretless poplar neck. I woodburned "Gov't Mule" on the fretboard and "Dr. Woody's Snake Oil" on the box. He loved it!

# CHAPTER 10: Cigar Box Preamp

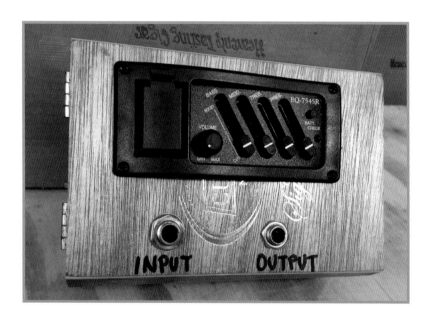

The Standalone Preamp Hack – The perfect companion for any homemade instrument toolbox. You'll get reduced feedback, deeper bass response, and it gets rid of piezo pickup ("fart box") tones for any instrument wired with a piezo pickup. It also enhances guitars with magnetic pickups by adding boost and EQ.

In one of our practices I was complaining about all the problems I had with instruments that used piezo pickups hardwired to an output jack. As stated elsewhere, *piezo pickups without preamps are nothing but fart boxes*. That's when the idea for this standalone preamp. It's deceptively simple: A $17 acoustic guitar preamp with a hacked input becomes a great EQ and signal

**PARTS:**
- Preamp and piezo rod kit* (page 46)
- ¼" (⅔ cm) guitar jack
- Empty cigar box that is deep enough to house the preamp
- 9V battery

*(*Note: a piezo rod pickup is included with the preamp. You'll need the wire from this!)*

**TOOLS:**
- Wire stripper or cutter
- Soldering iron and solder
- Coping saw, scroll saw, or Dremel rotary tool
- Black permanent marker or woodburning pen

Figure 10-1.

boost. And it's all housed in a cigar box! It's basically the same hack as the Foot Stomper plans, except that we're going to wire a ¼" (⅔ cm) jack instead of three piezo disks.

This is the perfect unit to boost the beer can mic. It also works great on any instrument that has a contact mic pickup without any signal boost.

Cut a 3½" x 1½" (9 x 3¾ cm) hole in the box to fit the preamp (Figure 10-1). You can use a coping saw, carpenter's knife, or a Dremel rotary tool with a cutting disk. I have a ⅗" (1½ cm) section of poplar that was a cut-off from a cigar box guitar neck that makes the perfect template for preamp routes.

Figure 10-2.

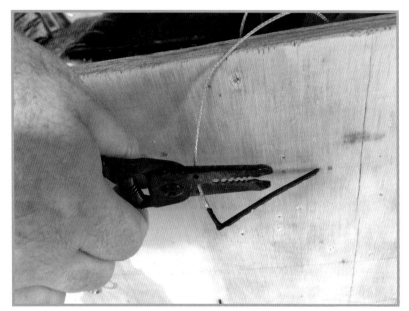

Figure 10-3.

Figure 10-4.

Drill two ⅜" (1 cm) holes in the box, one for each guitar jack needed (Figure 10-2).

Take the rod piezo out of the preamp packaging. Using wire cutters, cut off the rod piezo pickup from its wire (Figure 10-3). Cut closest to the pickup, leaving the longest length of wire possible.

Pull back the ground wire sheath to expose the lead wire. Strip off ¼" (⅔ cm) of the lead wire's insulation (Figure 10-4).

Solder the ground sleeve wires to the ground prong (the inner, circular portion of the jack). Solder the lead wire to the lead (Figure 10-5). This is now our hacked pickup wire and will become the input jack.

Figure 10-5.

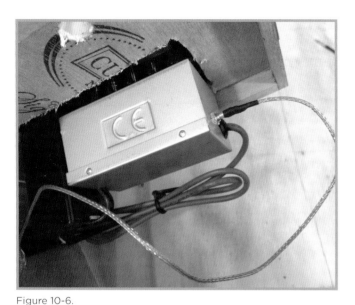

Figure 10-6.

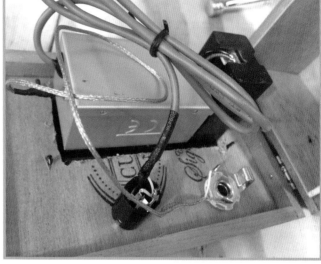

Figure 10-7.

Figure 10-8.

Insert the ⅛" (⅓ cm) plug of the hacked pickup wire into the receptacle of the preamp unit (Figure 10-6).

Install both guitar jacks to the cigar box. I would recommend positioning the hacked wire (input) on the right side of the layout and the black plastic jack (output) on the left side (Figure 10-7). Also, insert the 9V battery at this time.

Mark your input and output jacks accordingly (Figure 10-8). I used a Sharpie® marker, but you could use a woodburning pen or something more artistic.

ADDITIONAL NOTES:

- Unplug the guitar cables when not in use or it will drain your 9V battery.
- Dialing in the right tones is an *art*. Each instrument is different. The preamp is there to *sculpt* the tones and to also give signal boost to low-output piezos.
- If the instrument sounds too distorted, try dialing back the volume on the preamp and increasing the volume on the amp/PA system.

## Guitarcheology: Homemade Acoustic Guitar, Circa 1950

Although not a cigar box instrument, this is a fascinating piece of history that shows DIY ingenuity from a builder who desperately wanted to play guitar. The guitar dates back to the 1950s and features a body shape that was cut from a slab of stacked pine 1 x 6 (19 x 140 mm) boards. Birch plywood serves as soundboard and back, and a carved oak neck is glued in place.

The frets are improperly spaced, and although the builder cut 18 slots, he only installed six of the frets. (There are enough frets to play cowboy chords.) The headstock has six extra tuner holes, possibly drilled with the wrong size bit before the builder drilled new ones for the tuners.

# CHAPTER 11: Electric Washboard

*This feedback-proof design uses a magnetic pickup to capture vibrations of the corrugated steel face.*

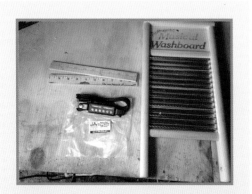

**PARTS:**
- Small washboard with a steel corrugated scrubber; antique washboards with brass or glass faces won't do
- Wood mounting brackets
- Acoustic guitar mounting tabs
- A cheap, low-profile sound hole pickup for acoustic guitars (For this example, I purchased one from *www. GoldFoilPickup.com*)
- An old yardstick or scrap pieces of thin wood
- Wood screws

**TOOLS:**
- Saw
- Drill and large drill bit

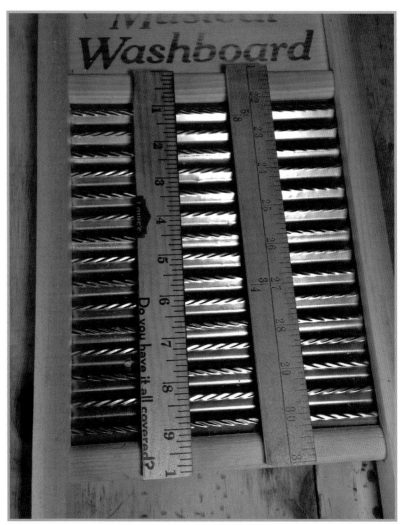

Figure 11-1.

A washboard is always going to be the loudest instrument in the band and rarely needs amplification. These things dominate any room. In fact, my washboard player, Ronn Benway, has been known to cover the underside of his scrubber with duct tape to quiet it down for certain bar gigs.

However, an amplified washboard is needed during large festival gigs when the rest of the band is fed into the PA system. The following design was created to give a feedback-proof instrument that can even be fed into delay and wah-wah pedals.

Overview: The setup simply calls for a magnetic pickup to be mounted on the back of the washboard, close to the corrugated steel, without touching it. The vibrations of the steel will be picked up just like a guitar string and fed into an amp.

Cut the yardstick into two pieces long enough to overlap the top and bottom wood mounting brackets, as shown (Figure 11-1).

Figure 11-2.

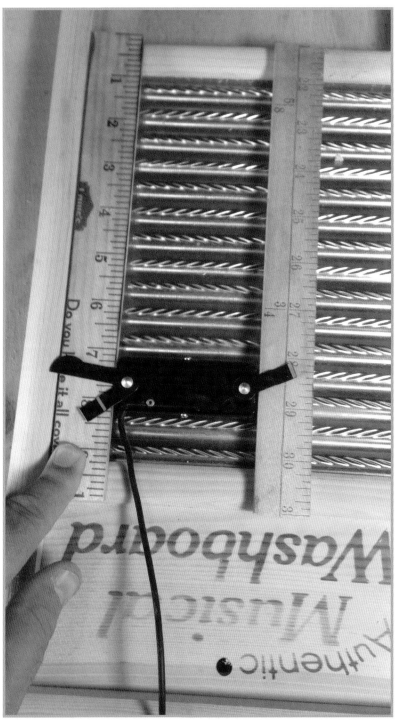

Place the yardstick pieces parallel on the work area and "mount" the pickup to them using the acoustic guitar mounting tabs. You may need to bend the tabs a little to make them grasp the yardstick. It should be placed approximately 2" (5 cm) from the bottom (Figure 11-2).

Place the pickup and yardstick assembly back on the washboard, face down, toward the steel (Figure 11-3).

Figure 11-3.

Figure 11-4.

Check to make sure the pickup isn't touching the steel. If it is, bend the mounting tabs on the pickup so that it's further away (Figure 11-4).

Drill pilot holes at the ends of the yardsticks and attach using wood screws (Figure 11-5).

Drill a hole in the faceplate of the washboard with a large drill bit (Figure 11-6). Feed the guitar jack through the hole (Figure 11-7).

The back of the washboard should look like the above image (Figure 11-8).

Drill holes in the washboard legs and insert rope as a strap (Figure 11-9). The washboard is upside-down when finished because the legs act as a perfect strap mount. They also won't poke into your hips as you play!

You can play your washboard with thimbles on your fingers or simply pick up a pair of spoons to scrub away. Many New Orleans players use the paint can lid keys that are given away at hardware stores.

Figure 11-5.

Figure 11-6.

Figure 11-7.

Figure 11-8.

Figure 11-9.

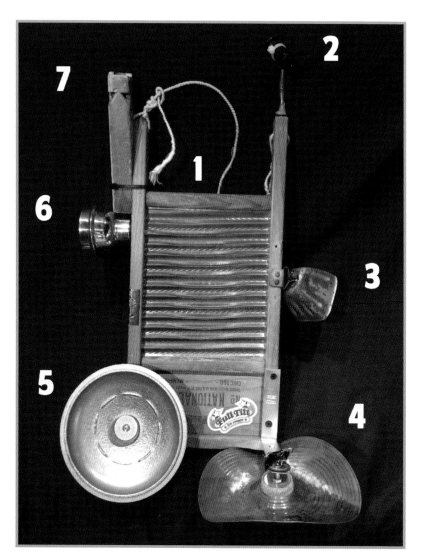

## Extra: Advanced Washboard Design in the Style of Ronn Benway

Ronn Benway's washboard contains bells, whistles, metal ashtrays, and other junk found at thrift stores. To play, he duct-tapes thimbles on his fingers before every show. (The thimbles will only last four or five shows before the tops are worn off.)

By the way, he really does dress like this. When he's in concert, Ronn becomes like Angus Young of AC/DC, dancing on the tables and running through the audience.

Just one example of the many washboards used and abused by Ronn Benway. The parts include:

1. An antique National #442 "Midget" Washboard by the National Washboard Company
2. Plastic wolf whistle mounted to the right leg with a doorstop spring
3. Toy cowbell
4. Splash cymbal (This one is completely destroyed after only three gigs!)
5. Metal pot lid
6. Cocktail shaker lid
7. Wooden train whistle

*Note: For festival stages and larger concerts, Ronn attaches two wireless tie-tack microphones to his rig, enabling all cymbals and accessories to be amplified in the PA system.*

Ronn plays his washboards with reckless abandon. The corrugated steel eventually gets worn away, sometimes flaking off mid-concert and cutting into his chest! His old washboards can be found on the walls of dive bars and clubs throughout America.

Every band needs a Ronn Benway.

PHOTO: FREDDIE GRAVES

Ronn Benway cuts loose when playing the washboard.

# CHAPTER 12: "The Lady" Guitar – An Electric Guitar Illegally Handmade inside a Prison

My guitar collection has grown so big, I had to open up a museum display at my father's blues bar, Speal's Tavern, in New Alexandria, Pennsylvania. The collection includes cigar box guitars from builders all over the world along with other examples of "poor man's guitars." Several of these instruments are showcased in this book.

One of my favorite instruments is a guitar that was illegally built within the walls of a state prison. I was lucky enough to meet the builder and learn the whole backstory on it.

"Junior Ben" didn't want me to mention his real name when I told him I was going to write about this guitar. He was still afraid of being called a "snitch" by other prisoners who helped him smuggle parts and illegally build this 23 years ago in the Huntington State Prison in Pennsylvania.

Prison life does that to you, even when you've been out for 17 years like Junior Ben.

This guitar is named "Lady," and the whole thing came to life inside the 126-year-old jail that is so ancient and massive, it is known locally as "The Wall." Junior Ben so desperately wanted a Les Paul Jr. "double cut" guitar during his incarceration, he began working with other inmates to secretly craft one in the back corners of the prison woodshop.

He had a neck from a broken guitar to start with. The heavy body was hand-carved from Pennsylvanian walnut and oak woods with white-painted binding. The hand-stamped brass truss rod cover has the word, "LADY," a tribute to "Lucille," the guitar played by his favorite guitarist, B. B. King.

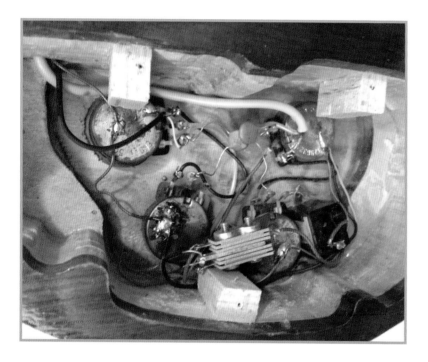

All the wiring was smuggled in from the prison shops or pulled out of headphone jacks that were still in the cells from the old days.

If you open the back control cavity, you'll notice that all the knobs are spaced very closely together, a necessary step in order to keep wiring to a minimum. Because Junior Ben worked the front desk at the prison, he was able to get pickups mailed to the prison and smuggled back to the shop. Unfortunately, he couldn't get the correct humbucker pickups to fit the routes and resorted to mounting single coils into the body, using black construction paper to cover the gaps.

To amplify it, he hacked an old G.E. Supertuner III radio and converted it into a guitar amp, although he had to make sure the radio still worked. If it was found to be altered, guards would confiscate it.

Think about all the secrecy that had to be maintained to bring this guitar to life! The wood had to be stashed somewhere in the woodshop during the whole process. The carving, routing, and setup had to be done when the guards were away. Scraps had to be hidden. How did they smuggle the wires? Other woodshop projects had to be slowed down in order to justify time spent in the shop. Incomplete parts had to have a hiding place during its construction. And once it was finally done, Junior Ben had to commit forgery to make prison documents saying the guitar was legally purchased outside the prison and mailed in from a family member. At any one point, the whole operation could have imploded by one bust from a prison guard. But it didn't. It survived.

The guitar spent five years in prison with him and was shipped home right before he was released in 2000. He continued to play this guitar for the next 13 years.

In 2013, Junior Ben sold it away to Guitars on George music store in York,

Pennsylvania. The owner, Jerry Duncan, called me because he knows I'm always searching for the next poor man's guitar.

Soon after acquiring it, I tracked Junior Ben down and we had a good afternoon together, talking about this guitar and his love for the blues. When I asked him why he sold the guitar away, he said, "My arthritis keeps me from playing music anymore. Besides," he continued, "this wasn't the first time I sold it. It was sold away several times in prison when I needed things." He looked at me with a sense of pride and bragged, "Its worth increased to 20 packs of cigarettes."

Twenty packs of cigarettes, indeed.

## The Cigar Box Guitar Museum inside Speal's Tavern, New Alexandria, Pennsylvania

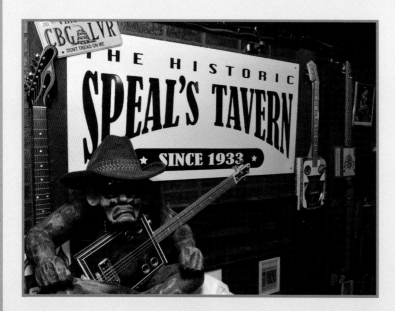

PHOTO: KEVIN STIFFLER

The perfect location for a Cigar Box Guitar Museum is inside a dive bar that hosts blues concerts and is located in the middle of a rural town. It also happens to be my father's bar, Speal's Tavern.

After years of collecting cigar box guitars from builders all over the world, my basement didn't have the space for me to cram any more instruments into it. I'd always had the desire open a museum so the public could experience them, too. Then in the fall of 2010, I got a phone call from my dad, Dan Speal, telling me that he decided to take over the small hole-in-the-wall tavern that had been in my family since the middle of Prohibition.

"I don't know what to do with this place," he said. "There's only three people here on a Saturday night. Nobody comes here anymore."

It only took a split second for me to blurt out, "I have an extra PA system that you can use to host live music." Then I added, "And I have a basement full of cigar box guitars that we can display as a museum!"

He loved the idea.

In October 2010, we had a grand re-opening of Speal's Tavern, debuting the Cigar Box Guitar Museum and announcing live blues music weekly. The museum collection, originally just 40 guitars, has grown to over 120 instruments in a rotating display. (Usually around 80 instruments are shown at any one time.)

PHOTO: KEVIN STIFFLER

PHOTO: KEVIN STIFFLER

*Acoustic Guitar Magazine* declared it one of the "Top 100 Places Guitarists Must See In America," placing the little dive bar next to the Martin Guitar Factory on the list!

The museum is open during bar hours. There's always live music every Thursday, Friday, and Saturday night.

## Speal's Tavern
*On the intersection of Rt. 119 and Rt. 22 in New Alexandria, Pennsylvania Open 3pm until 2am Tuesday–Saturday, www. Spealstavern.com*

# CHAPTER 13: Recreating Scrapper Blackwell's Cigar Box Guitar (A Builder's Diary)

Eric Clapton covered Scrapper Blackwell's song "Nobody Knows You When You're Down and Out" almost note for note. Rory Gallagher listed him as one of his biggest influences. Hell, even Robert Johnson turned his song about "sweet home Kokomo" into an ode about Chicago. But who remembers Scrapper Blackwell, the Indianapolis single-note picker who was sittin' on top of the world from 1928 to 1935?

As a cigar box guitar player, I had heard his name in the DIY circles as one of the blues greats who started on a cigar box guitar. Digging deeper, I found his final interview, printed in a 1960 issue of *Jazz Monthly Magazine*, just one year before he was murdered. In it, Blackwell described his first guitar:

*"Ain't nobody never told me nothin' in my life, never showed me anything. And the first guitar I ever had in my life I made it myself . . . Out of a mandolin neck and a cigar box. That's the truth, that's the truth. Put six strings on it and played it.*

*"When I picked up my first one I played. Not only played it but I made it."*
—Scrapper Blackwell, from his final interview, *Jazz Monthly Magazine*, 1960

During my search, I first wanted to find out about that cigar box guitar. Was he remembering the instrument correctly? It seems impossible to have a six-string guitar with a mandolin neck, I thought. So I found an old mandolin neck and an antique box and built one to find out.

I started with an old wooden cigar box and a 1920s mandolin/banjo neck. I chose

PHOTO: RANDY FLAUM

the banjo mandolin neck because it had the attached wooden shaft that goes through the banjo rim. This made the planning a lot easier. All I would have to do is cut holes at each end of the box to insert the shaft.

I made sure the neck was mounted with a small degree of back pull. That meant the shaft would be lower on the neck side and higher toward the butt end.

Once I got the holes cut out and filed neatly, I crafted a makeshift trapeze tailpiece from a 1928 license plate. (This is the same year his song "Kokomo Blues" was released.) The #5 on the plate approximates an "S" for Scrapper.

My next step was to use a Dremel rotary tool to make two primitive violin holes in

PHOTO: RANDY FLAUM

the box. I went with an "S" pattern again, using pictures of antique cigar box fiddles as inspiration for the look. (Yeah, I know Scrapper didn't have a Dremel back then, but I'm sure he wouldn't mind me cheating just a little bit.)

With the box now closed, I manipulated the license plate a little more, bending over the end to give it more strength. I then drilled the holes that would anchor the strings.

Since Scrapper's original cigar box guitar utilized a mandolin neck (which was probably an eight-string), but only had six strings, I knew I'd have two holes to cover up on this. I took an old sardine can and cut out a strip of metal to cover them up.

PHOTO: RANDY FLAUM

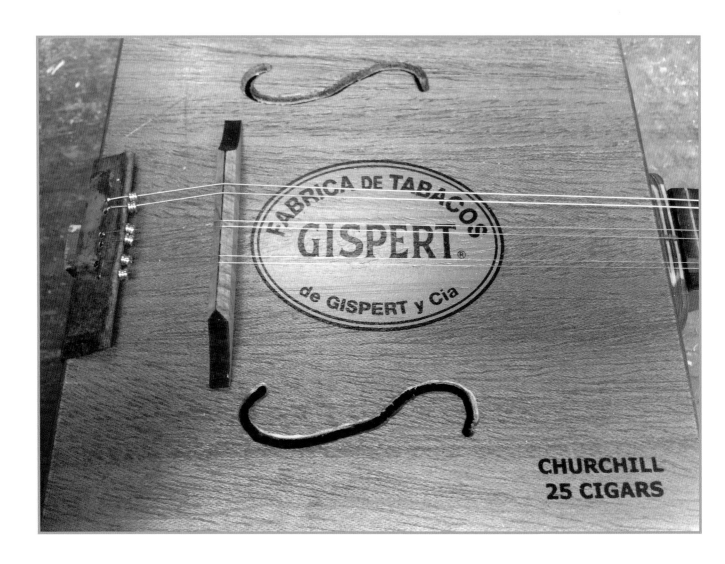

A set of letter punches allowed me to put "Scrapper" in the metal, creating a cool looking headstock.

A note on the tuners: I chose mismatched tuners to keep the primitive, homemade appearance.

Strings and Doubting Scrapper's Story: As I worked on this guitar, I constantly told myself that Scrapper's description had to be wrong. You just can't fit six strings equally apart on a mandolin neck and expect it to be playable.

I chose two wound G strings as the lowest strings. The rest of them were some extra high B and high E strings. I simply didn't want to exert too much pressure on this instrument by using thicker guitar strings.

When I first strung the guitar up, I doubled the strings like a mandolin, making it a three-string, double-coursed instrument.

The guitar played great and sounded great! *But* . . . this is not what Scrapper described! He didn't talk about playing a cigar box mandolin. He said "guitar" in his description.

## Guitarcheology: Discovering the Past and Recreating Legendary Instruments

My life as a cigar box guitarist not only seduced me into carpentry, it also intoxicated me with history. The more I explored the instrument, the deeper into the rabbit hole I fell. I kept finding musical byways, detours, and secret passages.

Cigar box guitars were more commonplace than I'd originally thought, with blues legends, lumberjacks, and average Americans building and playing them for their own enjoyment.

Over the years, I have collected antique instruments, old ephemera, and interviewed people about their cigar box guitars, each providing a new perspective and path to follow. This paths has inspired me to research the various forms of American music that were played on them. The end result is always the music.

So I decided to space the strings apart and tune it to an open blues tuning.

**The verdict**: Scrapper was right; it works! The tone is high pitched simply because of the short scale, but you can definitely play this like a six-string guitar. If you're a big guy like me, your fingers are going to be smashed together. A young kid like Scrapper, on the other hand, probably wouldn't have had any trouble.

# CHAPTER 14: Tips on Selling Cigar Box Guitars at Festivals and Craft Fairs

Do you want to learn how to be a millionaire, selling handmade cigar box guitars for fun and profit? Ha! Keep dreaming. However, you can make some extra cash vending these instruments at craft fairs, hometown festivals, and outdoor events.

These guitars pictured were just some of the 75 guitars I built just for one festival season. I had spent six months in preparation. Note the batch of six in the center served as a higher-end line to round out my selection. They were nearly identical to each other: same box, same pickups. This is a trait that allows me to optimize my time and resources during construction. The higher prices got sneers from some people and drove them toward the "bargain" guitars on the outer perimeter. By the end of the year, everything had sold, even the Expensive Six.

My 10 x 10 (3 x 3 m) vending tent is lined with nine old screen doors that are secured at the top and sides with plastic zip ties. The screens have been removed and replaced with hexagonal chicken wire, giving it an old fashioned look and allowing the guitars to be hung by the tuners. To keep the country look, I even bought some fake flowers from the dollar store and weaved them through the chicken wire, between guitars. I finished the whole presentation by lining the sides of the tent with cheap canvas painter's tarps that had big red circus stripes spray painted on them. The whole vending setup looked like it was from the 1920s.

This entire setup—the tent, guitars, and extra gear—all fit in my minivan. The screens are piled on top of the roof rack and held down with a ratcheting tie-down straps.

I've learned some rather good lessons about vending setups and scoping out festivals. If you enjoy building these instruments as much as I do, then you can find a festival or two (or more) this summer to sell your creations.

Here are some things to consider before becoming a guitar factory:

1. Demonstration is everything! The better you can play your instruments, the more you will sell. *Learn how to play your cigar box guitars before selling them.*

2. You're making DIY instruments. Fellow DIY people will most likely spend their time asking you questions on building so they can steal your ideas and make your own. It's okay, they're only a small percentage of the crowd. Befriend them.

3. This is not a job for recluses, hermits, or other people who don't like dealing with the public. You'll spend your entire day shaking hands, smiling, and talking to people. If you consider yourself a grumpy bastard, you're probably gonna have a bad time.

4. If you're planning on running a vending booth by yourself, you'll eventually burn out. Trust me, you'll be talking to multiple people at once, needing bathroom breaks, and finding it necessary to escape to eat and clear your head. Ask for somebody to assist you before booking your first show.

5. I repeat: The better you can play your instruments, the more you will sell.

## Preparation and Production

Lesson #1: You should be building cigar box guitars many months ahead in anticipation for a festival. In the past, my first fest would start on May 1. I started to build guitars in February in preparation for that fest.

Lesson #2: Build several guitars at a time.

If you want to optimize your time and resources, consider building guitars in "batches," much like baking cookies. For me, I have a particular guitar design that I developed and I strongly believe in. If I keep with this design, I can prepare a dozen necks at a time and then move on to boxes. I can also wire up a bunch of pickups in a separate step and keep them stored in my shop until I'm ready for them.

Building guitars in batches doesn't mean you're stifling your creativity. Each one can be unique. You'll just be optimizing your time and resources as you work on different areas of the guitar.

Lesson #3: Buy parts in bulk. You'll save a lot of money and always have the parts you need when you're ready for them. Guitar parts suppliers, such as *CBGitty.com*, give bulk discounts on certain parts, such as tuners, string sets, pickups, and preamps. Many parts are sold in lots of 12, so planning out a dozen guitars for each batch is a good way to start.

## Booking Festivals

Community arts and crafts festivals are a great place to sell cigar box guitars. Music festivals are even better because they have music lovers attending. Both are ripe for selling.

Tip #1: A great resource for finding fests in your area is *www.festivalnet.com*. This website not only gives you dates, locations, and times, but it also gives you contact and submission information for many of them.

I've used it to book fests and even shows for my band.

Tip #2: Try to book fests at least six months in advance. Craft vendors are a well-organized militia and always getting their applications early in for the next event. Because space is limited, you should apply early. Besides, it'll give you ample time to build a bunch of guitars.

Tip #3: Ask the event organizer if another cigar box guitar vendor will be selling. If so, don't book that fest. If there's one thing I've learned, it's that cigar box guitars sell great when you're the only one selling. If there are two or more cigar box guitar tents at a fest, you'll see your profits plummet. The simple fact is, people spend too much time comparing one guitar maker to another, and then suffer "death by over-choice" and walk away without purchasing. I just don't sell at events where other cigar box guitar venders are set up.

## Selling Extra Items

In addition to cigar box guitars, start thinking about extra items you can upsell to people who buy. These can be shirts, stickers, gig bags made from old denim jeans, and other accessories.

Selling your cigar box guitars at festivals is a lot of work, but it's also a lot of fun. You'll meet thousands of people, get to play in front of big crowds and, most importantly, you'll make some money doing something you love.

I never got rich from vending, but the income certainly helped my family in tough times. If you do things right, you'll find some success and personal satisfaction of your own.

## Essential Items You Will Need

1. Smartphone and a credit card reader, such as PayPal or Square. At the end of each fest, I discovered 50% to 60% of all my sales were via credit card. Make sure your cell phone is fully charged, too!
2. When you work a heavily attended festival, sometimes cell phone service suffers and you can't connect. Learn how to take down all credit card info the old fashioned way and take the slips home. You can then enter them into your cell phone app when you get home.
3. I made my signs huge and handwritten, giving a homemade look to them. Whether you go the primitive route or get the professionally printed, make sure they're nice and big so they draw attention.
4. A Roland MicroCube amp (or other battery powered amp) is a great way to demonstrate your instruments. If they don't have pickups, bring a microphone or stick-on pickup to plug in. Fests get loud and you want people to be able to hear your instruments.
5. Remember to bring a cooler filled with ice, water, sandwiches, and snacks since food at fests can get expensive. Also, you may get so busy that you just can't leave your tent, so a cooler is vital. You'll thank me later.
6. Don't forget to pack proper weights to secure your tent. You can't rely on the puny stakes that come with your tent. Bring some cement blocks or other types of weights to keep the whole store from blowing away.
7. Extra pens, pencils, sharpies, price tags,and zip ties are a necessity.
8. Bring a good attitude. (Grumpiness loses sales. Don't be one of those people.)

# Cigar Box Guitar and DIY Instrument Resources

In the last two decades, I have littered the Internet with information on cigar box guitars. I learned early on that any time I posted free information on these instruments, it would go viral. People are in love with DIY instruments, their history, and playing techniques. So here's just a quick handful of resources to help you dig deeper into the world of cigar box guitars.

*PoorMansGuitar.com* is the website we've built to contain supporting videos, lessons, and information from this book. Start here for video lessons and much more.

*ShaneSpeal.com* is my personal music website. Get all my concert dates, hear music clips, and find out what crazy things I'm up to next. Make sure to join the email list. My newsletters are not your usual band spam!

*YouTube.com/ShaneSpeal* is my video channel with free cigar box guitar lessons and building tips. I've been known to post one new lesson a day for two months in a row. Make sure you subscribe!

*SpealGuitars.com* features my handmade cigar box guitars that are for sale. Sure, there ain't nuthin' like playing a guitar you built yourself, but if you want an axe that I built in my tiny backyard woodshed, here's where you get it.

*StubbySlide.com* is my online store of guitar slides made for cigar box guitars, plus cool shirts and other "curious finds." I created the store because I couldn't find a good outlet for the slides I wanted to use in concert. It has grown into a music store that includes freakish guitar things resembling stuff you'd find advertised in the back of an old comic book.

*SpealsTavern.com* is the home of the Cigar Box Guitar Museum.

*CBGitty.com* sells new parts for cigar box guitar building, including Shane Speal brand guitar tuners and strings. They have parts, tools, and templates needed for building one or 1,000 cigar box guitars . . . and they're a really great bunch of folks, too. I help with their research and development to create new instruments, parts, and kits.

*SeymourDuncan.com/ wiring-diagrams* features easy-to-follow pickup wiring guides that are customizable to just about any configuration.

*CigarBoxNation.com* is the #1 social media website for cigar box guitars and DIY instruments. We've loaded it with more free plans, how to articles, photos, and more. Connect with the thousands and thousands of cigar box guitarists in the world. Attend cigar box guitar festivals and join in the entire community.

*CigarBoxGuitarParts.com* has great tips and articles on cigar box guitar building.

*BartHopkin.com* is the home of musical instrument inventor, Bart Hopkin. For years, Hopkin published *Experimental Musical Instruments Quarterly*—one of the greatest magazines on instrument creation, discovery, and plans. His PDF download of the complete back issues is essential to any builder who wants to dig deeper. He has also published many books on musical instrument design. I own 'em all.

*CigarBoxGuitar.com* is an online library of cigar box guitar music (in TAB format), history, articles, building tips, and more.

Unknown homemade instrument orchestra, circa 1940s.

Otto Rindlisbacher and his collection of homemade instruments from Wisconsin lumberjack camps.

*GuitarWorld.com* is the website of the world's biggest guitar magazine. Find my column, *The DIY Musician*, posted there.

*NOLAJazzMuseum.com* is the home of the New Orleans Jazz Museum, located in the Old Mint building right in the New Orleans's French Quarter. They're dedicated to preserving the history of New Orleans music, promoting its growth, and were a great help as I prepared this book.

*MIM.org*, the Musical Instrument Museum in Phoenix, Arizona, is the largest museum of musical instruments in the world. Their collection includes a Shane Speal four-string cigar box guitar.

*BarattoGuitars.com*, the home of Matty Baratto's Cigfiddle cigar box guitar. Baratto invented the paint lid resonator concept shown in this book. He's also outfitted some of the biggest names in rock n' roll with their own cigar box guitars. In fact, Paul McCartney and the surviving members of Nirvana won a Grammy for their collaborative song "Cut Me Some Slack" in which McCartney plays a Baratto Cigfiddle.

# Appendix

## 23" Fret Scale template

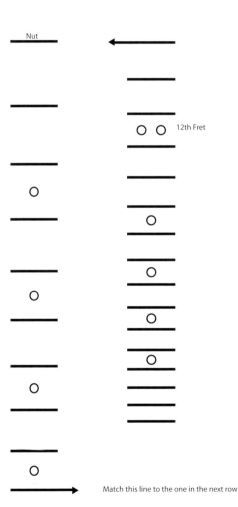

Nut

12th Fret

Match this line to the one in the next row

| FRET | DISTANCE FROM NUT |
|------|-------------------|
| 1 | 1.2" (245mm) |
| 2 | 2.5" (477mm) |
| 3 | 3.6" (697mm) |
| 4 | 4.7" (903mm) |
| 5 | 5.7" (1098mm) |
| 6 | 6.7" (1283mm) |
| 7 | 7.6" (1457mm) |
| 8 | 8.5" (1621mm) |
| 9 | 9.3" (1776mm) |
| 10 | 10.0" (1922mm) |
| 11 | 10.8" (2060mm) |
| 12 | 11.5" (2190mm) |
| 13 | 12.1" (2313mm) |
| 14 | 12.7" (2429mm) |
| 15 | 13.3" (2539mm) |
| 16 | 13.8" (2642mm) |
| 17 | 14.3" (2739mm) |
| 18 | 14.8" (2832mm) |
| 19 | 15.3" (2919mm) |
| 20 | 15.7" (3001mm) |
| 21 | 16.1" (3078mm) |
| 22 | 16.5" (3151mm) |
| 23 | 16.9" (3220mm) |
| 24 | 17.2" (3285mm) |

Photocopy template at 200%.

Get a free, printable version of this template at www.PoorMansGuitar.com.

# Index